Write Great Ads
A Step-by-Step Approach

Erica Levy Klein

Foreword by Bob Bly,
author of *The Copywriter's Handbook*

WILEY

John Wiley & Sons, Inc.

NEW YORK • CHICHESTER • BRISBANE • TORONTO • SINGAPORE

Library of Congress Cataloging-in-Publication Data
Klein, Erica Levy.
    Write great ads : a step-by-step approach / Erica Levy Klein :
foreword by Bob Bly.
      p.   cm.
    Includes bibliographical references (p.).
    ISBN 0-471-52418-2.—ISBN 0-471-50703-2 (pbk.)
    1. Advertising copy.   I. Title.
    HF5825.K49   1990
    659.13'2—dc20   89-27914
                                          CIP

Printed in the United States of America
      10 9 8 7 6 5 4

Printed and bound by Courier Companies, Inc.

••

Foreword

If you want to learn how to write good advertising—solid, sensible advertising that works—you've come to the right place.

Erica Levy Klein is an inspired teacher of advertising copywriting for two reasons.

First, Klein does not share Madison Avenue's obsession with aesthetics and creativity, but instead concentrates on honest, straightforward advertising—the kind that moves merchandise and makes the cash register ring.

Second, in this book, you don't just read about advertising theory; you learn by doing. You *write.* And that is the only way to gain real skill in copywriting.

Why am I so enthusiastic about this book? To begin with, I value Erica Levy Klein for her clear thinking, sensible approach and insights into what's *really* important in advertising.

Another reason is that it's concise and to the point. Too many advertising how-to books are ponderous tomes that take ten pages to make the single point that Erica makes in a paragraph. I admire her brevity. In today's information-overloaded society, Klein is one author who respects the busy reader's time, and this book provides a fast-paced way to learn the fundamentals of copywriting.

Most importantly, *Write Great Ads: A Step-by-Step Approach* doesn't just provide guidance and advice (although there is plenty of good advice in the book); it also takes you through the writing process and gets you writing—first just ideas, then headlines and concepts, then entire ads and commercials.

This is the only advertising book I know of that actually asks the reader to write, and I think it's a unique advantage. You can only learn so much by *reading* about copywriting. You learn the rest by doing. Some of the exercises are quick and easy; others take more time. All force you to think about products the way an advertising person thinks about them. Step by step, page by page, you learn how to write ads that sell.

There is something in this book for everyone, from casual readers who just want a basic understanding of copywriting or need to write an ad to promote their businesses, to the professional copywriters seeking to continue their education and hone their skills.

Many copywriters and business people are more word oriented than picture oriented, and when they write copy, it's with little concern for the visual aspects of the piece—a mistake in today's graphics-oriented society. Erica reminds us of the importance of words and pictures working together and provides helpful hints for making them do so.

Many of the lessons, tips, and techniques in this book are not available in other sources. Here you will learn billboard writing; rules for effective use of subheads; five easy steps to writing a brochure; secrets of successful direct mail; pitfalls to avoid when writing television commercials; the three basic types of radio commercials, and how to create them; "power words" for fund-raising and retail advertising; and much more.

Often a prospective client will call me to say, "I need a copywriter who is very creative and can write creative advertising." My answer is that, whether you are an advertiser or a copywriter, you should strive to produce advertising that is *effective*, not creative. This book will teach you how to write effective advertising. And if you can do that, you can make more money and achieve a greater level of business success than you ever dreamed of.

Bob Bly, author
The Copywriter's Handbook

Acknowledgments

Grateful acknowledgment is made for permission to reprint copyrighted material from the following books:

The Copywriter's Handbook, A Step by Step Guide to Writing Copy That Sells and *Secrets of a Free-lance Writer: How to Make $85,000 a Year* by Bob Bly, both published by Henry Holt and Company. And from *Ads That Sell: How to Create Advertising That Gets Results*, also by Bob Bly, Asher-Gallant Press.

Creative Newspaper, 11, copyright 1987, Newspaper Advertising Bureau, Inc. Special thanks to James H. Hollis.

And from the following agencies, companies, and organizations:

TBWA Kerlick Switzer. Special thanks to Susan Holmes and to the late Dan Kerlick, who was a better copywriter than I'll ever be.

Shoss & Associates Advertising, St. Louis, Missouri. Special thanks to Susan Christensen and Bill Shoss.

A.G. Edwards & Sons, St. Louis, Missouri. Special thanks to Tom Ptacek and Mary Atkin.

KRJY, K-JOY 96, St. Louis, Missouri. Special thanks to Dan Zarlenga.

KPLR-TV Channel 11, St. Louis, Missouri. Special thanks to Paul Vaughn.

Institute of Outdoor Advertising, New York, New York. Special thanks to Don Byer.

Ronald McDonald House, St. Louis, Missouri. Special thanks to Elisabeth Gutberlet and Susan Christensen.

American Red Cross, Bi-State Chapter, St. Louis, Missouri. Special thanks to Brian McDonough and Susan Christensen.

Kroll Advertising, St. Louis, Missouri. Special thanks to Ken Kroll, my favorite copywriter, for love, patience, and tolerance above and beyond the call of matrimony.

Contents

Introduction

I'll probably get kicked out of the Ad Club for saying this, but contrary to what this book's title implies, you do not have to write great ads—or even award-winning ads—to be a successful advertising writer (known as a *copywriter*.) In fact, you don't have to knock people's socks off with your creativity. If you know how to communicate what's important about what you're selling in an appealing way, you can boost sales, build greater awareness of your product or service, and have the boss eating out of your hand.

Did you know that all an ad has to do is sell, and it automatically qualifies as "great"? I kid you not. But here's even better news:

Whatever field you're in—or whatever your job title is—you only have to know a few advertising fundamentals to create simple but effective advertising that will do a good selling job and won't embarass you or your employer.

What's more, once you feel comfortable with these "building blocks" of advertising, you can rearrange them to create more complex forms of advertising such as brochures, direct mail pieces, and even radio and television commercials. The whole process of writing advertising can be quick, painless, and easy, despite what your experiences may have been up to now.

1

HOWEVER POWERFUL A MESSAGE IS, SOME PEOPLE MAY NOT BUY IT.

People have an overwhelming tendency to question what they're told. Even when it's cast in stone.

That's what makes us human. We make our own decisions. Sometimes right. Sometimes wrong. But always our own.

So it's hard to believe when people claim that advertising made them buy something they didn't want.

Sure, we'd like to think that the advertising we create has a powerful impact on you.

But the truth is we simply present facts. Try to make them interesting and entertaining. Then sit back and hope we got through.

As for having some kind of power over people's actions, greater forces than the advertising industry have tried.

And God only knows, no one does everything they're told.

ADVERTISING
ANOTHER WORD FOR FREEDOM OF CHOICE.
American Association of Advertising Agencies

Courtesy of *Creative Newspaper* 11. Copyright 1987, The Newspaper Advertising Bureau, Inc.

Consider the example set by a well-known, but inexperienced beginner.

God was probably the first advertising copywriter, and His only ad campaign was The Ten Commandments. They were incredibly effective; although they were written thousands of years ago, everyone still remembers them.

This was no miracle—not the advertising kind, anyway. After all, God knew His *audience* thoroughly and did plenty of on-site, firsthand research.

God also started with a reasonable *sales objective*: to lay down the law to the Children of Israel who were worshipping idols and generally behaving like wild party animals.

Next, after firmly establishing His sales objective, God developed a simple but effective way to communicate His most important ideas—an *ad* listing ten rules of order that everyone had to follow or risk eviction by the Heavenly Landlord.

Of course, since copywriters hadn't been invented yet, God lacked a catchy *headline* like "Slap Me Ten, Israelites!" or "Good God!" But the stone tablets did provide an attention-getting *visual* (the picture portion of an ad), and His *copy* (the written part) was clear, straightforward, and right to the point.

The combination of these two elements—visual and copy—became the *concept* God used to deliver His message powerfully and persuasively. (Having a great account executive like Moses deliver the Commandments probably didn't hurt either.)

I hope you'll enjoy *Write Great Ads* and that all of your advertising will get the same great reception as God's original "Top Ten Countdown." Just keep in mind the most important commandment of all: "Thou shalt not take thyself (or advertising) too seriously." Advertising was never meant to be treated as a religious experience despite what you may have heard from various holy admen and women. Instead, it's something to be done to the best of your ability, in the spirit of adventure, using whatever gifts the world's First Copywriter has generously bestowed on you.

1.

●●

Take Advertising One Step at a Time

There are a lot of great "how-to-write-advertising" books out there: thick, serious books written by experts (and semi-experts) filled with tales of "how I created that brilliant ad campaign," "how I made that ho-hum product sell like hotcakes," and "how the client actually got down on his knees and kissed my hand in gratitude." Unfortunately, all of these advertising books are distressingly alike. They give you the ground rules for writing advertising, bombard you with dozens of do's and don'ts, and then leave you on your own to sink or swim in an ocean full of doubts. The authors never seem to stick around long enough to make sure you understand what to do—and in what order—so you can experience similar success writing advertising yourself.

It's my hope that *Write Great Ads* will provide just the right amount of step-by-step guidance when you're first trying to write advertising, especially if it's not part of your regular job description or if you don't have any formal training in advertising.

Call it hand-holding if you will, but I'm a great believer in learning by having someone *show* you what to do first and then *imitating* him or her until you figure out how to do it yourself. You have my mother to thank for this educational philosophy. My father always told her that I wouldn't amount to anything if she kept writing my English compositions for me, but fortunately Mom knew that *the majority of people learn better by following someone else's example than by being lectured to*. (Take a bow, Mom!)

That's why this book is short on sermons from the mount and long on opportunities to practice writing advertising. By doing the easy (and hopefully enjoyable) exercises in each chapter, you'll begin writing effective advertising faster and be able to point proudly to professional results sooner. Even if you don't believe you're an especially good writer, *Write Great Ads* can help you create convincing, persuasive advertising in just a matter of hours. This is especially helpful if the deadline was yesterday and your boss wants to know why the ad you promised her isn't on her desk already.

Although this book is designed to help anyone who wants to start writing advertising immediately, I think its monkey-see, monkey-do approach will prove especially helpful if you are

- *An employee* in a company where you occasionally (or more than occasionally) have to write advertising copy.

- *A small business owner* who has to write your own advertising materials because of budget limitations or because you simply don't have the time to teach a freelancer everything about your product or service.

- *A salesperson* who has to turn out sales literature or advertising materials in a hurry.

- *A student* who's interested in entering the copywriting field.

- *Someone who already works in another area of advertising* and wants to know more about the writing side.

The fact is, advertising is not a lofty art; it's a vocational skill, just like woodworking, welding, or plumbing. (So what if the kitchen sink exploded the last time you tried to repair a faucet!) All it takes to begin writing advertising is a solid grounding in the basics; then you can meet any reasonable and clearly defined sales objective.

Remember, your advertising efforts don't have to be the world's greatest or win a bunch of awards. They can just be "okay" or "passably good" and still perform well—probably even better than the slick advertising created by professionals who don't know your product, service, or cause half as well as you do.

2.

· ·

Beat the "Maybe I'm Not Creative Enough" Blues

I have always believed that we're all born with more or less the same degree of creativity. Over time, because of pressures to conform from parents and schools, we lose a lot of that natural ability because we're trying so hard to be like everyone else.

A lucky (or is it crazy?) few hang onto their built-in creativity for dear life and become writers, artists, musicians, dancers, and actors. But everyone else—or so it seems—battles constant insecurities about whether they're creative enough to do any type of creative work.

If you're in this latter category, and you suddenly find yourself having to, or wanting to, write advertising, the worst thing you can do is worry about whether you're creative enough to cut the mustard. You'll immediately become so tense and anxious about "making the grade" that you'll block out all kinds of good ideas or dismiss others before they've had a chance to fully develop. Instead, focus on telling yourself that everyone has hidden reserves of creative ability and that all you want to do is tap yours to the fullest extent. Since advertising is a bit of a con game anyway, I don't have to tell you how important confidence is to mastering the basics.

The Real Difference Between Success and Failure

If nothing I've said convinces you, and you're still concerned about your "creativity quotient," consider what most creative professional people know but rarely share with outsiders: It's okay to fail creatively—not just once but a thousand times. It's okay to come up with creative ideas the people laugh at, sneer at, or otherwise hack to pieces. It's okay to fall flat on your face again and again, and to write words that don't convince anyone to do anything else other than to go to sleep. Immediately.

But what's *not okay* is giving up—allowing a sense of personal failure to convince you that you were never creative in the first place, and you might as well throw in the towel before anyone finds out.

Everyone is creative—including you. The most important difference between creative professionals and everyone else is that professionals give themselves permission to fail, to go down in flames with an idea. But once that fire is out, they light another spark and another and another until they come up with something that feels good to them—or at least better than the last thing everyone else hated.

Here's another secret of creative professionals: We don't censor ourselves as early or as often as everyone else. We don't get an idea for an ad and immediately tell ourselves, "Oh, forget it," "That's stupid," or "That'll never work!" Even if our initial idea doesn't seem like the right one, we keep thinking about it because often it's a steppingstone to a much better idea.

In other words, we tend to give almost every idea a fair hearing no matter how "wacko" or far out it seems at first. A famous advertising poster from Rapp & Collins, a New York direct marketing agency, lists 99 "idea killers" including everything from "The last guy who came up with that isn't here any more" to "You've gotta be kidding!" The list concludes (very wisely) that, "No idea is born perfect. Give it a chance to grow."

Being supportive of yourself is very important and tends to play a major role in personal, as well as professional, success. So before you read on or do any of the exercises in this book, promise yourself that, no matter what, you're not going to waste time worrying that you might be a failure creatively. After all, you've got better things to do, like thinking of a good idea, getting something on paper, and polishing it until you're reasonably happy with it.

Persistence is the key to writing advertising, and for that matter, to any other pursuit you care about.

Warm Up Your Creative Muscles

One of the things that makes people feel so un-creative when they face an advertising project is what I call "deep brain freeze." It's hard to start writing or even gathering information when your brain is like an ice-cold car engine in the dead of winter.

The best solution is to warm up your brain gradually with a few "brain games" that are totally unrelated to the project at hand. This way, you'll be killing two birds with one stone. You'll skillfully avoid the work you have to do, and at the same time, you'll trick yourself into relaxing and allowing your creativity to surface.

Here's a great exercise for limbering up in anticipation of any advertising assignment—simply because it has nothing to do with advertising and will allow you to stall for five whole minutes.

EXERCISE ••••••••••••••••••••••••••••••••••••

How Do I Love Thee Magnets, Let Me Count the Ways

Take five minutes and, in the space provided, write down all the ways you can think of to use small powerful magnets (each about the size of a quarter). Don't be concerned that what you come up with sounds a bit strange; the purpose of the game is to flex your creative muscles.

You might consider using the magnets "instead of rivets in steel buildings." Another idea might be to use them "as stacks of poker chips that won't fall over."

If you own this book, feel free to use the blank spaces below to write down your ideas. But if this is a book from the library, kindly resist the temptation. Otherwise, you may find the librarian hitting you over the head with an unabridged dictionary . . . which may increase your height, but only temporarily.

Are you ready? Remember: List everything you can do with small magnets the size of a quarter. On your mark . . . get set . . . GO!

Time's up. Congratulations! As a result of all your original ideas, you've earned an honorary degree in magnetology. Now all you have to do is stay away from anything metal.

3.

··

Homework, Legwork, and Research: How to Avoid Copy That Doesn't Sell

Despite what you have been told—or what you may have imagined—advertising writers don't just sit down at the typewriter or word processor and begin to type out a dazzling stream of words. First, they do their homework by gathering as much information as possible about what they're selling ... and even more important, *who* they're selling it to.

If you're like most people, you probably want to skip over this admittedly boring step and get right to the exciting writing part. Unfortunately, that will only get you into a heap of trouble later on. You see, advertising isn't really a result of inspiration like many other forms of creative writing you may be familiar with.

> *Advertising is only effective if it sells. And that means preparation is much more important than inspiration.*

Think of it as the difference between real grapes and wax ones. Real grapes (like real ads) are plump, sweet, juicy, and full of the information people want to know about your product or service.

Wax grapes are what you get when you don't bother to dig for the specifics or fall back on empty superlatives, clever phrases, or glitzy showmanship. You end up with a waxy mouthful of vague and meaningless copy. And not surprisingly, people spit your ad out in a hurry because it just doesn't say anything. You've harvested wax grapes, because *no ad sells unless it informs*.

According to advertising copywriting guru Bob Bly, there's a simple way to avoid the infamous Wax Grapes Syndrome. When you finally sit down at the typewriter to begin writing, your file of background information should have at least *twice as much material as you'll end up using in the final version of your ad.*

Bob wisely recommends taking the following steps before you type a single word.

Get All of the Previously Published Material About What You're Selling

For an existing product (the same goes for a service or cause) that might include

- Tear sheets (published copies of previous ads)
- Informational brochures
- Annual reports
- Catalogs
- Article reprints
- Technical papers
- Copies of speeches or announcements
- Copies of sales presentation materials
- Audiovisual scripts
- Press kits or press releases
- Market research
- Advertising plans
- Sales reports
- Letters from users of the product
- Back issues of newsletters
- Files of competitors' ads and literature

Even if the product is new, remember that the birth of every product is followed by a baby carriage full of paperwork, such as

- Internal memos
- Letters spelling out technical information
- Product specifications, blueprints, plans
- Illustrations and photos of product prototypes
- Engineering drawings
- Business and marketing plans
- Reports
- Proposals

The next step is to look over this material so you can sound half-way intelligent when you . . .

Ask Questions About the Product

- What are all the things it promises to do for the buyer?
- Which of these promises is the most important?
- In what ways is the product used?
- What are the characteristics of the product?
- How is the product different from the competition's? (What does it offer that is either exclusive or better?)
- If the product isn't different, what attributes can be stressed that haven't been stressed by the competition?
- Does the product make use of any special technology?
- What problems does the product solve in the marketplace?
- How is the product currently being advertised or marketed as compared to competing products?
- How does the product work?
- How reliable is the product? How long will it last?
- How efficient is the product?
- How economical?
- How much does it cost?

- Is it easy to use and maintain?

- Who purchased the product and what do they say about it?

- What materials, sizes, and models is it available in?

- How and where can consumers buy it (or is it delivered by the manufacturer)?

- What service and support does the manufacturer offer?

- Is the product guaranteed?

Finally, try to pretend you're a potential buyer—a real live, flesh-and-blood human being. Put yourself in the shoes of the person you'll address your advertising to, and

Ask Questions About Your Audience

- Who is most likely to buy this product?

- What exactly does the product do for the buyer?

- Why does the consumer need the product? And why does he or she need it now?

- What motivates that buyer?

- What is the customer's main concern when buying this type of product? Is it price, performance, reliability, quality, efficiency, or availability?

- What type of person is the product selling to right now?

- Does the advertising have to appeal to more than one audience at a time? (A toy ad, for example, must appeal to both the parent and the child.)

Now I know why people call Bob Bly the Lieutenant Columbo of advertising! He's always asking one more question so he can be sure he's rounded up all the right facts (and all the usual suspects). Because in copywriting, *specifics* sell.

EXERCISE •

Your Boss' Nephew

Your boss' favorite nephew has just called you in a panic because he needs help with an ad he's writing for his graduate school communications class. (How this kid even got into graduate school anyway is a mystery to everyone.)

The ad should announce that the top-selling toothpaste is now available in piña colada flavor—a development that the manufacturer hopes will attract more adult buyers. Because this kid's a bit dense, he doesn't have any idea where to start looking for the information he needs. He has one month to complete his advertising project.

Take five minutes and come up with *three kinds of people he could possibly call or talk to to get the information he needs.*

One example might be a local reference librarian who can help him get general background information about toothpastes. Another might be the marketing manager at the toothpaste company.

Now you give it a try—after all we're talking about the boss' nephew here, and maybe Mr. Big will remember your eleventh-hour save of his favorite relative at salary review time. Think of three people the boss' nephew could bother for information about a new piña-colada-flavored toothpaste and write them down here.

1. _____

2. _____

3. _____

Helpful Hint: If you're thinking of telling him to interview dentists, competitors, and adult toothpaste users, you're on the right track. But if you're thinking of telling him to interview people ordering piña coladas at the local bar, think again.

4.

● ●

I've Got This Ad to Write—Now What?

After the research stage there is a natural tendency to feel like Lucy and Ethel in the chocolate factory with too much information and no clear idea of what to do with it all. It's often especially difficult to decide what's important enough to include in your copy and what's not.

Before you write any advertising, keep in mind the six stages you'll probably go through in developing and organizing your research:

1. *Preparation.* This is the stage where you collect all the initial information and do your homework thoroughly so that you can avoid the infamous Wax Grapes Syndrome (see Chapter 3).

2. *Frustration.* Next comes the understandable feeling that you're overwhelmed by all the information you've collected, and you have no idea where to begin. Many people give up at this stage and think they don't have what it takes to write advertising. All they really need is a little extra P & P: Push and Patience.

3. *Incubation.* This is when you start to shuffle through the information and try to make connections between the various things you know about the product. You'll do some initial concepts combining a headline and a visual—or

decide whether to do a copy-only ad. (Don't worry, you'll learn all about developing concepts in the next chapters.) You'll mull over what you know and take some time to clarify it in your mind. You may also get incredibly frustrated at this stage because nothing much is happening ... or because you can't think of anything original. You may even want to give up. But don't—the fun stuff is just about to begin.

4. *Illumination*. Suddenly, like a light bulb going on over your head, you'll think of a half-decent idea. Perhaps two previously unrelated elements connect in a new way, or you'll think of something you hadn't thought of before. You'll take the plunge and begin to generate some more ideas in rough form. Maybe they're nothing you're happy with yet, but at least you're rolling—the creativity is starting to flow.

5. *Evaluation*. This is where you stand back, take a deep breath, and review what you've come up with so far. You decide whether they are good ideas or not. You're critical of your ideas, but in a positive way. Maybe you pick out the best one.Or if you don't like any, you come up with some new ideas, or variations, or a way to take the initial idea one step further.

6. *Elaboration*. At last ... the final stage! This is where you slug it out with your ideas, fine tuning and revising them so the copy and the visual (if there is one) work together effectively. It may take several hours (or days) to get this stage right, but don't lose hope—it comes with the territory. What's more, it keeps getting easier the more you do it. Honest.

EXERCISE ••••••••••••••••••••••••••••••••••

The *Reader's Digest* Condensed Version

Here's a great way to slog through the quicksand of the treacherous Frustration stage and get yourself on track for the joys of Incubation, Illumination, Evaluation, and Elaboration (not to mention Exultation).

This five-part exercise will help you review your research and focus on the most important point (or points) you want your ad to communicate to your target audience.

When you feel you've learned as much as you can about your product or service (or one you choose for the sole purpose of this exercise), get comfortable in a quiet room.

1. Using as few words as possible, start by telling your imaginary buyers all the ways your product (or service or cause) will help them meet their important emotional or physical needs.

_____

_____

_____

_____

_____

_____

_____

Quick Shortcut: If you're stuck, start by thinking about how the product makes the consumers feel better about themselves. Will it make them feel sexier, smarter, or more confident? "Feel good" advertising is generally very effective because it deals with the ego first and the intellect second.

2. Once you have a list of reasons why someone should buy your product or service (or donate to your cause), ask yourself *which is the most powerful, most desired benefit?*—the one that strikes you as more important than the rest.

This will be your *major benefit statement*—the one message you must communicate about your product in order to get people to buy it.

3. If you want a friend to try this product, *what one statement could you make about the product to attract attention and encourage your friend to find out more?*

_____

_____

_____

_____

_____

In print advertising, this will be the basis for your *headline.* (In radio or TV, this information would form part of your *opening segment.*)

Helpful Hint: Just to help get you started, an example of a headline for a wrinkle cream might be, "Prune-Away will make you feel 10 years younger in 10 minutes."

4. Now imagine that you are writing your friend a letter about the product. *What supporting details could you give your friend to provide enough reason to buy the product?*

_____

_____

_____

_____

_____

_____

_____

_____

_____

These details will be the basis of your *supporting claims*—the information (and features of the product) you will use to prove that what you've said in your *major benefit statement* is really true.

Helpful Hint: Examples of supporting claims for Prune-Away would be that it was formulated by a team of mad Swiss scientists, approved for testing on higher life forms by the FDA, and that a famous countess swears by it. Or at it, depending on whether it's working that day.

5. Finally . . . *How would you get your friend to actually take action? To get up out of that comfortable chair and go to the store or pick up the phone and make a buying decision?*

_____

_____

_____

_____

_____

This will be the basis of your *closing arguments* and your *call to action*—your last chance to get your potential buyer to act.

Helpful Hint: An example of closing arguments combined with a call to action would be "Prune-Away is available for a limited time only at $2 per jar." (Or at least until the manufacturer can get rid of the putrid stuff.)

With this five-part exercise, you have begun to make sense of the information available to you and are well on your way to writing advertising.

Now all you have to do is think of the best way to dramatically present this information, and that's done with a concept.

5.

●●

Develop a Concept

Developing a concept means coming up with a visual and a headline that work together so well that *they're more powerful together than they would be separately.* The best kind of visuals complement the theme of the headline and catch the reader's eye so that the person reads what you've written instead of turning the page. (In TV commercials, the concept means something slightly different. It's the story or specific execution the writer uses to get the selling message across, and that means it's very often strongly visual in nature.)

In the simplest terms, *a concept is the delivery of your message in some unique, memorable way.* The secret of developing good concepts is to dramatize your benefits—to make them spring to life in a way that captures people's interest and imaginations.

I've filled an entire legal pad just trying to find the right concept for an ad—but the results were usually worth it. When I went with my first impulse—a top-of-my-head concept—it usually turned out to be something ho-hum because I didn't keep going and try for something really special, unusual, or different.

If you're like many people, you probably think developing concepts is a waste of time; you're anxious to get going—perhaps so you can get the whole thing over with. You'd also probably rather get into the project first and then decide later what visual to use.

Frankly, I used to develop concepts this way myself. After I'd finished every word of copy, I'd go back and think of what visual might be a good match for what I'd written. Then my creative director encouraged me to give up my evil ways and develop my ideas for the visual at the same time I was thinking about my main selling idea and my headline.

As much as I hate to admit this, he was right. The results really are a lot better when the major visual and the major idea are created at about the same time. Somehow, "striking while the iron is hot" means you tend to come up with a visual and copy that are more in tune with each other than if you wait until after you've written every word of copy and then try to retrace your steps. Perhaps it's because, your original spark of inspiration may have died out or may simply be flickering. So, try to develop your visual and your headline simultaneously. It will really make a difference in the final results.

EXERCISE ••

Take a Mental Breather

Before you tackle your first concept, take a moment to look over all your research one more time. It may seem unnecessarily repetitive (and a major bore besides) but knowledge of your product (or service or cause) will give you the power and confidence you need to create the most effective concepts.

Expanding on the information from your five-part "*Readers Digest* Condensed Version" exercise in Chapter 4, take the next 15 minutes to briefly jot down:

1. A complete physical description of your product (size, color, materials, cost, etc.).

_____

_____

_____

_____

_____

_____

_____

_____

2. What you think the prospective buyer gains from buying your product. A more attractive appearance? Greater financial savings? Pride in being the first to purchase something new and exciting?

_____

_____

_____

_____

_____

3. How you're going to back up your claims. Readers or viewers won't just take your word for it that your car gets better gas mileage than a competitor's—you'll have to be ready to prove it.

_____

_____

_____

_____

_____

_____

_____

_____

4. What motivations or special inducements you're going to use
to get your reader to respond.

_____

_____

_____

_____

_____

_____

_____

5. Anything you'll use to enhance the reader's perception of your
product, including:

- What you'll offer to minimize feelings of risk, such as a
  money-back guarantee, a warranty, or a certificate of
  authenticity.

_____

_____

_____

_____

_____

• Any attractive financial terms such as the ability to use charge cards, financing, time payments, volume pricing, or trade-ins.

• Options—choices of sizes, colors, styles, or accessories.

Now carefully review all of this information and assign a number from one to ten according to how much emphasis you think each point deserves.

The good news is that there are no right or wrong answers; different people can have widely different interpretations. Your job is simply to organize the information according to what you—and others you trust—think is best for the time being. The idea here is to give yourself a starting point. You can always change your mind later—and probably will.

Helpful Hint: This bears repeating: When you're trying to decide what is really important to a buyer (and what to hang your hat on), think of what matters to the person *on an emotional level* first. It's usually more important for someone to get a raise out of the boss than it is to save the company the same amount of money, for example.

EXERCISE ••

Your First Print Concept

Now take a deep breath and plunge into the deep end of the pool. It's time to try out your first concept for a print ad. (A *print ad* is any ad that appears in a newspaper, magazine or publication.)

Start with any size sheet of paper or use the spaces below. On the left side, write out a description of what you feel is the best way to *visually* sell your product. On the right side, jot down some rough idea of the most important thing to say *verbally* about your product.

You'll learn how to create a headline in the next chapter, but for now, don't worry if what you have doesn't sound like a real ad headline. You should have just enough to give you a general idea of what you want to say and serve as a starting point.

An example of a *visual* for an ad selling a cruise to Hawaii would be:

A photo of a ship surrounded by a giant flower lei.

An example of the most important thing you want to say *verbally* in your ad would be:

This is the only cruise that you can take to Hawaii for under $1,000 per person.

Most people have more trouble thinking of a visual for an ad than determining what is important to say. So, courtesy of Bob Bly's excellent book *Ads That Sell,* here are nine suggestions for developing visuals fast without tearing your hair out:

1. *Show a picture of the person who provides the product.* Frank Perdue put Perdue chickens on the map this way, and discount broker Charles Schwab helped catapult his firm into national recognition. The power of this technique is that it enhances people's trust in a company . . . they can see the face behind all the promises.

2. *Make the product your hero.* In this approach, the ad is illustrated with a close-up photograph of the product against a plain background, which immediately gets the subject matter of the ad across to the readers. A variation of this theme is to show a close-up of the product in its package. This familiarizes the readers with your packaging, so when they go to the store, they will notice it and reach for it on the shelf.

3. *Show the product in use or the benefit of using the product.* If you're advertising toothpaste, don't show toothpaste on a brush; show white teeth. If you're advertising a gas-fueled portable grill, show a happy family having a backyard barbecue.

4. *Show the end result of the product.* If you're selling a pasta maker, don't show the machine; show a delicious plate of ready-to-eat linguini carbonara. If you're advertising a desktop publishing software package, don't show the software; show a beautifully designed, computer-generated newsletter or report.

5. *Show before and after.* This is an old standard, but it is still powerful because it works. For a hair replacement product, show before-and-after pictures that demonstrate how the product gave a bald man a full head of hair.

6. *Illustrate your main point with a diagram.* In industrial, high-tech, or product ads, always consider using a diagram to add visual interest. Technical people respond well to visual information presented in the format to which they're accustomed. For instance, accountants like spreadsheets, computer programmers like flowcharts or samples of programs, civil engineers like blueprints, and architects like architectural drawings.

7. *Depict a life style.* This approach creates visual interest by allowing the readers to see themselves in the ad. For example, an ad appealing to busy business executives might show an executive working late at night in the office, surrounded by a blizzard of paper. Ads for cigarettes, gourmet foods, and other life-style products often depict yuppies and yuppy puppies (their junior counterparts) or other types of people the advertiser believes are the market for the product.

8. *Build credibility with a testimonial.* In a testimonial ad, a customer is speaking in his or her own words about a product, service, or cause. If possible, always show a picture of the customer for an added degree of credibility.

9. *Go with an all-copy approach.* In ads that are all copy and contain no visual, the headline becomes the major visual focus.

Now that you know these quick shortcuts to coming up with visuals, try sketching out the basics of your first print concept below. Use a household cleaning product you're familiar with that's newly available in Spring Rain fragrance, or choose one from your imagination.

The Visual for My First Concept Is

_____

_____

_____

_____

_____

_____

Helpful Hint: If you're thinking of visuals like a bottle of household cleaner with an umbrella sticking out of the cap in the middle of a spring rain, you're on the right track. Don't be afraid to be literal or obvious. More sales are lost by being too subtle than by hitting your audience over the head with the sales message.

The Most Important Thing I Want to Say in My First Concept Is

_____

_____

_____

_____

Helpful Hint: Consider a starting point like, "This household cleaner works just as well as other cleaners, but smells fresh—like spring rain." A less successful starting point might be, "This household cleaner smells like something that got left out in the rain."

Tired of all this preparation? Be patient. There are still two more things you need to know before you develop your first concept. The first is *the difference between features and benefits;* and the second is *the anatomy of an ad.* They're both important in getting you comfortable with the process of writing advertising, and in the next two chapters, you'll learn everything you never wanted to know about both.

6.

● ●

Feature Creature Versus Benefits Champ

My favorite boss, Kitty Vance, taught me the difference between *features* and *benefits* my first day on the job. She said, "Features just lie there like a sleeping dog. Benefits are what happens when the dog gets up and licks your face."

That was Kitty's way of saying that *features* are the characteristics of a product or service that are "built-in" when you buy it—in other words, "the things it already comes with." A special permanent press setting is already part of a washing machine when you buy it, for instance. That means it's a feature.

A *benefit* is what the buyer gains from the features. To put it another way, *it's what the feature does.* If something is part of a product's general description, it's probably a feature. But when a feature gets translated into a specific outcome, it becomes a benefit. And benefits are what primarily motivate people to buy—although features are also important. Features not only prove the benefit is true, but enhance the buyers' feeling that the product or service is genuinely valuable.

For instance, the benefit of a washer's special permanent press setting is clothing with fewer wrinkles. As a result, your clothes look better and you feel better about wearing them. Perhaps you even feel more attractive to the opposite sex. These are all considered benefits, and as you can see, they may be based more on internal perceptions than on external reality.

In advertising, *it pays to promise a benefit that is unique to what you're selling and that no one else is currently talking about.*

That can be difficult sometimes because there are so many similar products out there. But the more you know about your product and its competition, the easier it becomes.

Sometimes there simply is no real competitive benefit. (Cosmetics, perfumes, liquor, and cigarettes are all notorious for this.) In these cases, you really have to dig deep to make your concept appealing enough so it *seems* to promise a competitive benefit even if there really isn't one. (Now you know why it's so hard to tell all those ads for makeup apart!)

EXERCISE ••

Make Benefits Your Feature Attraction

In the left column, list all the features your product, service, or cause offers. In the right column, translate these features into *benefits* that will be meaningful to or attract buyers.

If you're publishing a new travel magazine for people over 50, one feature could be that the magazine is "printed every other week." The benefit is that "readers get current travel information sooner than they would in a monthly magazine."

Now it's your turn to try. Choose your own product or service . . . or think of your most recent stereo or TV purchase.

FEATURE	BENEFIT

Helpful Hint: Remember, people don't buy "things"; they buy what the things will do for them.

A Word About People's Real Needs

Keep in mind that when you are developing benefits of any kind, what you're really trying to do is affect people's emotions. So concentrate your efforts on making the readers (or viewers or listeners) realize exactly how your product, service, or cause meets one or more of the basic emotional needs that all human beings share:

- *Life*—with appeals to safety, security, health, and saving money.

- *Love*—with appeals to the desire to love and be loved and to enjoy sexual fulfillment.

- *Bodily comfort*—with appeals to being warm, nourished, saving work, enjoying a relaxing atmosphere, and being free from stress.

- *Personal importance*—with appeals to status, ego fulfillment, and the desire for success, power, and respect.

- *Sense enjoyment*—with appeals to sight, hearing, smell, taste, and touch.

7.

•••

The Anatomy of an Ad

Once you have a concept that includes a possible visual and the most important thing you want to say, it's time to flesh it out (no pun intended) and develop the complete anatomy of the ad.

Just like the human body, an ad has its own anatomy. And from head to toe, each part of your ad plays an important role:

- The *eyes* of an ad are its *visual*—the graphic hook that catches the readers' interest in the first place.

- The *voice* of the ad is its *attention-getting headline* —the most important thing you want to say about your product, service, or cause—that convinces your readers to go further for more information.

- The *body* of the ad delivers the details of the complete *selling message* and proves your case. This is also the *heart* of your ad—the place where you share the *benefits* of your product, service, or cause in a way that produces maximum emotional response.

- The *feet* of your ad are where you get some form of commitment to spend, send, call, or attend. You are providing *closing arguments* and *calling for action*—getting the readers up on their feet to take the next step toward your product or service.

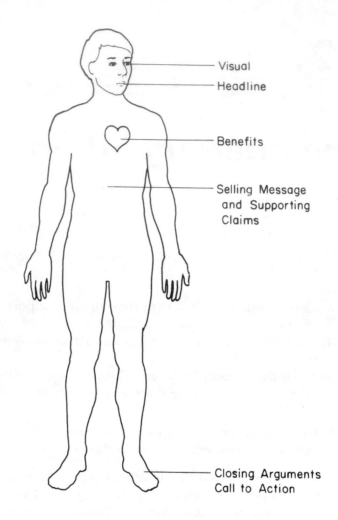

Visual

Headline

Benefits

Selling Message
and Supporting
Claims

Closing Arguments
Call to Action

Anatomy of an ad
Illustration by Lisa Cheuk

EXERCISE •

Fleshing Out Your Concept

Using the rough concept you developed in Chapter 5, briefly state
what you think you'd like to say in each part of your ad. If you'd
rather develop a completely new concept, think of how you would
promote your favorite restaurant.

EYES

A Description of My Visual Might Be:

_____

_____

_____

_____

Helpful Hint: Think of what you like most about something. A good visual for a restaurant might be delicious sample dishes or smiling service people.

VOICE

The Most Important Thing I Want to Say in My
Ad (the Headline) Might Be:

_____

_____

_____

_____

Helpful Hint: Think of what you'd say out loud to someone you were trying to convince to visit your favorite restaurant. Would you talk about the great food, the low prices, or the hip and trendy people who hang out there?

(optional) *Something of Secondary Importance*
that Doesn't Necessarily Belong in the Headline
but Deserves to Be Emphasized (in a Subhead)
Might Be:

_____

_____

_____

_____

_____

Helpful Hint: What's something important but not absolutely essential to say about your favorite restaurant?   That it offers diners a barbecue special every Tuesday? Or perhaps that it hasn't been closed down by the health department yet?

BODY/HEART

The Supporting Claims that Back Up *and* Prove
the Most Important Thing I Want to Say Might Be:

_____

_____

_____

_____

_____

_____

_____

_____

_____

Helpful Hint: Think of specific reasons why someone should risk a trek across the urban landscape to eat there. Lola the luscious waitress probably won't win over diners as well as food that won't require a trip to the emergency room.

FEET

My Closing Arguments or Call to Action
Might Be:

_____

_____

_____

_____

_____

_____

_____

_____

Helpful Hint: Gentle persuasion will always work more effectively here than implied threats from the Baseball-Bat-Wielding Salvino Brothers.

8.

••

Create the Headline

If you have to choose one part of your ad to work on the hardest, make it your headline. If your headline doesn't do its job in communicating the most important benefit and presenting it in a clear, bold, dramatic way, the time you spend on the rest of your ad is virtually wasted.

According to Bob Bly, there are eight basic types of headlines, although there are an infinite number of combinations:

1. The *direct headline* simply says what you want to say in the most straightforward way, but with a little extra enthusiasm. *Example:* "Pure silk blouses—30% off for one week only."

2. The *indirect headline* arouses curiosity and forces you to read the body copy to get the real message. *Example:* "Lemon." (This famous ad for the Volkswagen Beetle captured reader attention by appearing to criticize its own product.) Figure 8–1 shows an example of an indirect headline.

3. The *news headline* focuses on recent changes or developments. *Example:* "Announcing the new colors of Clarion cosmetics!"

4. The *"how-to" headline* explains ways to do something that readers want to know. *Example:* "How to stop smoking in 30 days—the secrets of success!"

Very funny, Mrs. Lenzen.

You had to do it, didn't you, Mrs. Lenzen.
You couldn't be like the 250,000 other people who finally gave up trying to
stain their free sample of Wear-Dated® Carpet with StainBlocker.℠ Well, you got us.
Wear-Dated Carpet does not prevent holes caused by battery acid. But thanks to people
all across America who tested our carpet against *their* toughest stains, we can
now say Wear-Dated Carpet with StainBlocker offers stain protection never
before available. And thanks to you, Mrs. Lenzen, we also have to
suggest that everyone keep their car off the carpet. For now.

℠ Wear-Dated is a registered trademark of Monsanto Company

Figure 8–1
Courtesy of TBWA Kerlick Switzer

5. The *question headline* arouses curiosity. Sometimes question headlines can backfire if readers don't really care about finding out the answer. *Example:* "Is your air conditioner costing you more than it should?"

6. The *command headline* tells your prospects exactly what to do. *Example:* "Aim high. Buy New Horizons basketball shoes."

7. The *"reason why" headline* is self-explanatory. *Example:* "Six reasons why you should join the American Aerospace Institute."

8. The *testimonial headline* lets the customers do the selling for you. *Example:* "I won a million dollars playing the Illinois Lottery!"—Joe Layton, Centralia, Illinois.

Research studies prove that five times more people will read your headline than will read your body copy. Naturally, that means your headline has to instantly telegraph what you want to say in simple language that anyone can understand. Readers will not stop to figure out what you're trying to say; they'll simply turn the page, and you will have lost them forever.

Bob Bly presents the four functions of a headline:

1. *Get attention*

2. *Target the audience*

3. *Deliver a complete message*

4. *Draw the reader into the body copy.*

Here are two more things to remember as you write headlines:

• *Headlines of ten words or longer sell more effectively than short headlines.*

• *Headlines that promise a benefit sell more than those that don't.*

To generate a headline quickly and easily, simply answer these three questions:

1. *Who is my customer?*

2. *What is the most important benefit of this product? (What will make the customer want to buy it?)*

3. *What are the features (or offers) that will help support the major selling benefit and convince the customer to take the action I want.*

From there, it's simply a matter of arranging this information in clear, compelling, and interesting terms. If your headline makes the reader take notice and want to know more about your product, then you've done your job well.

EXERCISE ••••••••••••••••••••••••••••••••••

Become a Headliner

Here's your chance to practice writing each of the eight basic headline types.

1. Make a list of words and benefit phrases that you feel somehow relate to your product—the more the better because you'll have more to choose from later. You may find some useful descriptions in the power word list on pages 49–50. If you don't have a specific product in mind, imagine a new peach-flavored natural soda with no sugar or caffeine called Peach Fizz.

_____

_____

_____

_____

_____

_____

_____

_____

_____

_____

_____

_____

_____

_____

_____

_____

_____

_____

_____

Helpful Hint: Words and benefit phrases for the peach-flavored soda might include: pure, fresher, 100% natural, no caffeine, no sugar, bushels, tastes like an orchard, fuzz and thirst-quenching flavor.

2. Mix and match the words from this list to form the eight types of headlines discussed.

Direct

_____

_____

Example: "Discover an orchard full of flavor in every sip of Peach Fizz."

Indirect:

_____

_____

Example: "It's a peach."

News:

_____

_____

Example: "Announcing a new peach-flavored soda with bushels of thirst-quenching flavor."

How-to:

_____

_____

Example: "How to enjoy true peach flavor with no sugar and no caffeine."

Question:

_____

_____

Example: "Why settle for anything less than pure peach flavor in a soft drink?"

Command:

_____

_____

Example: *"Get more peach fuzz per square inch. Drink Peach Fizz."*

Reason Why:

_____

_____

Example: "Here's why Peach Fizz takes the peaches."

Testimonial:

_____

_____

Example: "I drink Peach Fizz because it reminds me of the orchards I used to play in."—Dwight Larson

Power Words

If you're ever stuck, you may want to combine these "power words" with words and benefit phrases that relate to your product to create headlines in a flash.

You	Just
Free	Modern
Imagine	Dramatically
Proven	Switch
Easy	Success
New	Comfortable
Introducing	Go

Announcing
It's here
At Last
Just arrived
How to
Why
Sale
Quick
Bargain
Last chance
Guarantee results
Save
Powerful
Fast
Now
Revolutionary
Picture
Deserve
Unique

Call
Built
Advantage
Experience
Explore
Sample
Visit
Enjoy
Meet
Learn
Do
Breakthrough
Latest
What
Idea
Available
Great
First

9.

● ●

Billboard Writing: Copywriting at 55 Miles per Hour

One of the most enjoyable things you can do with your newfound skill of matching a headline to a visual is to create an attention-getting billboard for your product, service, or cause. With a billboard, visuals count more than copy because if the graphics don't grab people at 55 miles per hour, they probably won't pause to read your copy either.

So let your imagination run wild as you think of a big, bold graphic that will dramatize the major benefit of your product. Then think of any sentence (or two brief sentences) of one to ten words that will communicate that benefit with pizazz.

To get you started with this exercise, let's look at some examples of Obie-Award-winning billboards from the Institute of Outdoor Advertising.

Figure 9–1 is a standard-size billboard that incorporates a one-dimensional visual and several words of copy.

The billboard in Figure 9–2 is oversized and effectively uses a visual extending beyond the confines of the usual rectangle to add extra impact.

Figure 9–3 is even more eye-catching—a three-dimensional, inflatable billboard that literally and figuratively pops out at you. (The inflatable car gets "wrecked" and "repaired" every 30 seconds.)

Figure 9–1
Courtesy of the Institute of Outdoor Advertising. Client: Fischer Packing Company. Agency: Doe-Anderson Advertising, Louisville, Kentucky.

Figure 9–2
Courtesy of the Institute of Outdoor Advertising. Client: British Airways. Agency: Saatchi & Saatchi, Compton, New York.

EXERCISE •

Billboards-While-U-Wait

First, think of an annual event in your town. Then, choose one of the types of billboards mentioned previously and, using the rectangle provided as a starting point, create your own visual and headline to advertise the event.

Figure 9–3
Courtesy of the Institute of Outdoor Advertising. Client: Custom Auto
Body. Agency: Innis-Maggiore-Olson, Canton, Ohio.

10.

· ·

Subheads—
The Underrated
Secondary Headline

There are several good reasons to use a subhead in addition to a major headline in your ad. Although the "sub" in "subhead" makes it sound like it always goes under the headline, a subhead can also be used as a lead-in for the headline. Although the use of a subhead is strictly optional, it can come in handy when there isn't room to say everything in the headline.

A subhead can help you:

- *Expand on the major benefit in the headline* by adding specific information. For example, a headline might read, "The Bendix automatic factory door saves you time, money, and headaches with every delivery." The subhead might read, "Now save 50% when you order before August 1."

- *Bring out an additional point* that didn't fit well into the headline or that deserves special emphasis. The headline might read, "Announcing the sale of the century at all Woody's stores!" And the subhead might read, "Enter to win a cruise to Disney World!"

- *Serve as part of a one-two punch* that begins with the headline. The major headline might read, "What should a caring mother do about diaper rash?" And the subhead might answer, "Absolutely nothing. The cure is built right into the diaper."

One of the nice things about subheads is that you can make them longer than your headline. Subheads generally tend to be more explanatory, while the headline is more telegraphic.

EXERCISE ••••••••••••••••••••••••••••••••••••

Subhead, Subhead, Where For Art Thou Subhead?

Take one of the headlines you developed in the previous chapter's "Being a Headliner" exercise and create a subhead that expands on the major benefit, brings out an additional point, or serves as the final shot of a one-two punch.

My Headline Would Be

_____

My Subhead Would Be

_____

Helpful Hint: If your headline for the peach-flavored soda was "It's a peach," then the subhead could build on that idea and suggest specific benefits by saying, "No sugar. No caffeine. No kidding." A less successful headline/subhead combination might be: "Drink Peach Fizz. Or else."

Would the subhead introduce the headline or follow it?
(   )Introduce   (   ) Follow

Why?

_____

_____

11.

● ●

Sexy Body Copy

Your body copy gives you a chance to prove that whatever you're promising in your headline is actually true.   You'll do this by combining the supporting evidence you've gathered in your research with relevant benefits and important features.

Body copy is the trickiest part of writing any type of advertising because you have to tell your story and stay true to the spirit of the headline at the same time. For instance, if the headline is serious in tone, your body copy has to continue in the same tone as you prove your case with specifics.

The best way to write effective body copy is to analyze your headline (and subhead, if you have one). Then, keeping in mind the example your headline sets, simply continue "talking" about your product or service in the same voice. All you have to do is "tell" your story enthusiastically to imaginary listeners using all the information you think would convince them to make a decision to buy.

When you read over what you've written, remember to make sure your sentences flow smoothly from one to the other. Also try to be sure that what you've written sounds confident and compelling enough to make someone take action. To spice things up a bit, you may want to use some tricks of the trade (see Chapter 15) such as using sentence fragments or beginning a sentence with a preposition.

When you're done writing, check your copy's readability by having someone you trust read it over and give you their honest opinion about whether they hear any "snags." Or, if you don't feel brave enough to take that step, read the copy into a tape recorder and play it back to yourself.

Quick Tips for Rewriting Body Copy

After you've finished writing body copy, put it aside for a while (preferably overnight) before rereading it. Pay particular attention to your headline and the first few sentences in your body copy— also called the *opening*. Most openings are overwritten because you were probably just getting warmed up when you wrote it. Your opening must be immediately interesting, involving, and informative, and you must pack the most meaning into the fewest possible words. If you haven't already done so, try to create a rhythm and flow in your copy and sustain it for the rest of the ad.

Now go on to the *middle* of your ad and review it to make sure your sentences and phrases support your sales message clearly and persuasively.

Finally, at the *end* of the body copy make sure you tie up all the loose threads and satisfy your readers' need for a strong close. Go out with a bang—not a whimper.

EXERCISE ·······································

Body Double

Try editing this choppy copy for smoother flow and greater reader impact. Again, there are no right or wrong answers—only what you think sounds better when your "mind's eye" reads it over.

Clean Up Your Act Now with Webber . . .

Contamination can cost you more than you would have ever thought was possible. It can cost you time and money and labor too. And, your reputation if you're not careful. Before this happens, consult Webber. We have a unique and effective approach for getting microbiological contamination under control before it controls your lab. We take your bio-burden extremely seriously. Call Webber today at 1-800-555-1212.

Helpful Hint: Start by taking out any unneccessary punctuation or words, as in the sentence, "It can cost you time and money and labor too." Then work on how sentences begin, such as the sentence, "And, your reputation if you're not careful."

12.

Accentuate the Positive

This seems like a good place to encourage you to avoid writing negative (or ho-hum) copy. Strongly positive copy always gets better results.

Here are a few don'ts that will prevent you from falling into this all-too-common trap:

- DON'T try to sell your product by bad-mouthing the competition. You won't look good in comparison, and (horrors!) people may even sympathize with the competition and buy their product instead. This is the equivalent of scoring a touchdown for the opposite team, and you don't want to have to face the coach after doing something that dumb.

- DON'T discuss "downer" topics like pollution, inflation, or recession unless your product can actually do something to change them. No one wants to read depressing copy—your reader will tune you out and switch to something more pleasant.

- DON'T make readers concentrate too long on an undesirable situation before presenting them with a way to cure or avoid the situation.

EXERCISE ••••••••••••••••••••••••••••••••••

Things Are Looking Up

Try turning a negative headline into a positive one:

For example:

> *Before Acme Forklifts our safety record wasn't a pretty picture.*

can be turned into

> *With Acme Forklifts our safety record is the picture of success.*

Now you try it. Turn this negative headline into a more positive one:

> *You can't get a better mortgage for your needs.*

Helpful Hint: A positive headline is like giving someone a direct compliment. It sounds a lot better to say "I think you're great" instead of "I think you're not all that bad."

Now do your own *negative* and *positive* version of a headline for your product or service ... or for that Rolex watch you've had your eye on.

My Negative Headline

My More Positive Version

13.

· ·

Closing Arguments/ Call to Action

Even if you are successful in communicating benefits and building confidence in your product, it won't do any good unless you convince your readers to take the desired action.

This doesn't necessarily mean that your readers have to open their wallets and buy right this second; sometimes you just want to start the wheels turning in the right direction. But the object is clearly to make the prospects do something. Without a *call to action*, all your efforts may be wasted.

Here are a few ways to make your prospects act sooner instead of later by peppering your copy with powerful motivators:

1. *Offer incentives*. A free gift, a product sample, or a money-back rebate can all be effective.

2. *Give a deadline*. "This offer will expire on March 31. So hurry!"

3. *Make it easy to respond*. Use a toll-free 800 number.

4. *Mention that quantities are limited* and that orders will be filled on a first-come, first-served basis only.

5. *Offer quantity discounts*. "Buy two and get a third one free!" "Spend $100 or more, and qualify for a free gift (or credit coupon)."

6. *Give a money-back, no-risk guarantee.* "Satisfaction guaranteed or your money will be cheerfully refunded."

Whatever *closing arguments* or *call to action* you use, think of the end of your ad as a ribbon that ties everything together and makes the entire package more appealing. As the final installment in your sales message, it should provide a memorable conclusion and ask for the order.

EXERCISE ··

Closing Thoughts

Write a call to action that encourages your buyers to call or return the coupon to get the *Electric Utility Update* mentioned in the following ad. Keep it to two or three sentences at most.

Important information about

Electric
Utility
Stocks

If you own electric utility stocks, A.G. Edwards can put timely information at your fingertips with our *Electric Utility Update.*

Each issue contains an industry outlook and highlights current developments that could affect your investments.

The latest issue of *Electric Utility Update* is available at no charge.

_____

_____

_____

_____

Helpful Hint: Never let readers or viewers guess what they have to do to take the action you want. Tell them in very specific terms to clip a coupon, make a phone call, or visit a specific office.

14.

• •

Showtime! Put It All Together and Write Your First Ad

Now it's time to build on everything you've learned and construct your first complete ad. According to Bob Bly ("The Unofficial Census-Taker of Copywriting"), there are 32 different flavors of ads out there—just one more than Baskin Robbins.

- The *question ad* asks a question in the headline and answers it in the body copy.

- The *quiz ad* presents a quiz for the readers to take. Their answers determine whether they are prospects for the product or service being offered.

- The *news ad* announces a new product or something new about an existing product.

- The *direct ad* provides a straightforward presentation of the facts.

- The *indirect ad* has an obscure headline designed to arouse curiosity and entice the readers to read the body copy.

- The *reward ad* promises a reward for reading the ad.

- The *command ad* commands the readers to take action.

- The *price and where-to-buy ad* announces a sale, describes the product, gives the price and discount, and tells where to buy it.

- The *reason why ad* presents some or all of the reasons why the readers should buy the product.

- The *letter ad* is an ad written in letter form.

- The *before-and-after ad* shows the improvements gained by using the product.

- The *testimonial ad* features a user of the product or a celebrity speaking out in favor of the product.

- The *case history ad* is a detailed product success story.

- The *free information ad* offers a free brochure, pamphlet, or other information. The ad concentrates on getting the readers to send for free literature rather than on selling the product directly.

- The *story ad* tells a story involving people and the product.

- The *"new wave" ad* relies on far-out graphics or offbeat copy to grab attention.

- The *reader identification ad* uses the headline to select the audience.

- The *information ad* gives useful information relating to the use of the product in general rather than pushing the product directly.

- The *location ad* features the product used in an unusual location to highlight its versatility, usefulness, convenience, or ruggedness.

- The *fictional characters ad* centers around a fictional character such as Mr. Whipple or The Jolly Green Giant.

- The *fictional places ad* emphasizes a fictional place such as Marlboro Country or Bird's Eye Village.

- The *cartoon or cartoon strip ad* uses everything from simple stick figures to complex, highly sophisticated graphics.

- The *meet-the-advertiser ad* has the advertiser appearing in the ad to speak about his or her own product.

- The *invent-a-word ad* coins a word to describe a product or its application.

- The *comparative ad* shows how your product stacks up against the competition.

- The *challenge ad* challenges the readers to find a better product than yours.

- The *guarantee ad* focuses on the guarantee, not the product.

- The *offer ad* focuses on the offer and the sale, not on the product.

- The *demonstration ad* shows how the product works.

- The *pun ad* uses the headline to attract attention with clever word play. The pun is explained in the copy.

- The *contest or sweepstake ad* offers an opportunity to win prizes or money.

- The *tie-in-with-current-events ad* brings timeliness and urgency to the selling proposition.

EXERCISE ••••••••••••••••••••••••••••••••••

The Whole Enchilada

Choose one of the 32 types of ads listed and write a short but complete ad for your product or service. If you don't have one in mind, try writing a half-page magazine ad for a new vegetarian enchilada at Margarita's Mexican Drive-Thru.

Make sure you include the three essential elements from the anatomy of an ad: headline, body copy, and closing arguments/call to action. For extra credit, you might want to try writing a subhead.

Helpful Hint: If you feel frozen and don't know where to start, try one of the following fast-track exercises to warm up.

EXERCISE ••••••••••••••••••••••••••••••••••

Adver-doodling

When you first start writing a magazine or newspaper ad, the most important thing is to stay relaxed. One way to make the whole process more fun is to tell yourself you're only "doodling."

First, write down benefits, boastful statements, puns, word plays, and situations that are related to your product, service, or cause. After you've doodled around for a while, let your mind play with some visual ideas.

Next, try some experimental headlines. Before long, you may even have something you like. At least you'll be past the staring-at-blank-paper-in-horror stage.

EXERCISE ••••••••••••••••••••••••••••••••

The Inside Outline

Another way to ease yourself into writing a print ad is to create an outline. Outlines have gotten a bad rap because everyone remembers them from grade school. Actually, they're another good way to take the fear out of getting started.

If you're going to use this particular approach to "The Whole Enchilada" or an actual advertising assignment, your outline should contain:

- A headline

- Introductory copy or, at the very least, the direction you want to take in the ad

- A subhead if you're going to use one

- What you consider the most important supporting claims

- A description of your visual if you're not going to have a copy-only ad

- Any closing arguments or call to action

Helpful Hint: It might also help you to sketch a rough layout (an indication of how you think your ad should look that contains some of the most important copy).

15.

• •

Gear Up to Write a Longer Ad

How do you decide whether you're going to write a long ad or a short one? A lot depends on the product and what there is to say about it. Some products—such as cars, computers, stereos, insurance policies, investment opportunities, courses and seminars, cruises, cameras, and home exercise equipment—have numerous features and benefits.

Others—including soft drinks, fast food, some package goods, jewelry, cosmetics, lingerie, pet food, and shampoo—don't necessarily lend themselves to a lot of supporting claims.

The length of copy also depends on the audience. Some customers don't need a lot of information and are not accustomed to reading long text. Others, including many business readers, seek out all the facts they can get and will gladly devour as much as you give them.

The third factor in determining copy length is the purpose of the copy. If you want the copy to generate a sales lead, then there's no need to go into complete details because you'll get a chance to provide more information when you respond to the lead. On the other hand, an ad that asks for the order by mail must provide all the facts the readers need to make a buying decision and order the product.

According to Bob Bly, the copy should contain enough information—no more, no less—to convince the greatest number of qualified prospects to take the next step in the buying process. If you're unsure of how long to make the copy, you're better off including too much information than not enough.

Copywriters use a number of stylistic techniques to pack a lot of information into a few short paragraphs of smooth-flowing copy. Here are just a few tricks of the trade that may help:

- *Keep all paragraphs as short as possible.* Develop a new paragraph about every four to six lines of set type.

- *End with a preposition.* It adds to the conversational tone of the copy. A nice little bonus is that it lets you take revenge on your English teachers.

- *Use sentence fragments.* They help keep your average sentence length down. And sentence fragments can add drama and rhythm to your copy.

- *Vary sentence length.* This will help you to obtain a better flow of words and improve your pacing.

- *Begin sentences with conjunctions.* Not exactly your English teacher's favorite convention, but beginning sentences with "and," "or," "but," or "for" makes for a smooth, easy transition between thoughts. Conjunctions can often substitute for longer expressions such as "nevertheless," "notwithstanding," "conversely," "equally important," "moreover," and "furthermore."

- *Use one-sentence paragraphs.* An occasional one-sentence paragraph provides a change of pace that can liven up a piece of copy. When all sentences and paragraphs are pretty much the same, the reader gets lulled to sleep. A one-sentence paragraph is like a sudden curve in the road. It can shock your readers into wakefulness again.

- *Use bullets, breakers, and numbers.* Make use of numbered,

  1. First item
  2. Second item
  3. Third item

  lettered,

  A. First item

B. Second item

C. Third item

or bulleted

- First item
- Second item
- Third item

lists of brief key points. This divides the copy into short, manageable sections. Besides making the copy easier to read, it also makes it easier to write.

- *Use mechanical techniques for emphasis* (but sparingly). Many readers skim copy without reading it carefully, so an underline or highlight can be useful in calling out key words, phrases, paragraphs, and selling points.

Here is a list of just a few of the mechanical techniques copywriters use to call attention to key words and phrases in longer ads, brochures, and direct mail:

Underlines

Capital letters

Indented paragraphs

Boldface type

Italic type

Colored type

Fake handwriting

Arrows and notes in the
    margins

Yellow highlighting

Reverse type (white type on
    black background)

Boxed copy

Callouts

Postscripts (in letters)

EXERCISE ••••••••••••••••••••••••••••••••

Smoother Sailing

Using at least three of the techniques mentioned in this chapter, turn the following hard-to-wade-through longer ad into one that's easier on the eyes and the brain.

Switch from an IRA to an Annuity
and Collect Your Rewards!

The new tax law has eliminated the deductibility of IRA contributions for many investors. If you're looking for an alternative to accumulate money for your retirement, an annuity may be the answer. There are many benefits: Annuities offer the same tax-deferred accumulation advantages. Annuities do not have a maximum yearly contribution—you can place as much money as you wish in an annuity. With annuities, there's no co-mingling of pre-tax and after-tax dollars. Variable annuities offer a variety of investment options. Fixed annuities offer a variety of investment options. And unlike IRAs, annuities don't have to be withdrawn at age 70 1/2. They can be left tax deferred much later than 70 1/2, usually until age 85.

And when you do need the income, you can convert your annuity so that it starts paying you monthly checks. You can choose to receive your checks for a specified period of time, say 10 or 20 years, or even for life. Consider how an annuity can aid you in your retirement planning. Write for more information today.

Helpful Hint: Start by using bullets to separate the key benefit statements and work from there.

My Reworked Ad Reads Better Like This:

_____

_____

_____

_____

_____

_____

16.

∙ ∙

Now, Tackle a Brochure

After learning how to write an ad, the next step is to try writing a brochure. Why? Because after mastering the basics of ad writing—headlines, subheads, support statements, closing arguments, and calls to action—you're ready to build on them to write more extensive copy. Don't tell anyone I told you this . . . but a brochure is actually just a long ad in a slightly different format (see Figure 16–1).

What's a brochure all about? Like an ad, it's a printed bulletin designed to sell (or help sell) a product to potential customers. The only difference is that a brochure must give a fairly complete description of the product and provide the customers with more of the information they need to make an intelligent buying decision.

There are other strong similarities between an ad and a brochure.

An ad has a headline that communicates a powerful sales message.

The cover of a brochure—whether it carries a headline or just a title—must also do a strong selling job.

An ad usually has a prominent, eye-catching graphic.

Brochures should also have well-chosen graphics (especially on the cover) that clearly identify the product and what it can do for the readers. Ideally, a brochure should also contain a photo graph or drawing that shows at a glance what the product is, how it is being used and, if possible, the end result the product will produce. Always show rather than tell in a brochure. Make use of graphs, photos, charts, tables, diagrams, schematics, and other visual aids to tell your story (Figure 16–2). And remember that one large photo is better than several tiny pictures.

An ad has to contain descriptive support copy that fulfills the promise of the headline.

And so does a brochure. In the first few lines of descriptive copy (or in a subhead), be sure to outline the major benefits or advantages of using the product.

And, finally, an ad has to incite action, and so does a brochure.

Although you'll read many brochures that are strictly explanatory, they are most effective when they conclude by asking the

Introducing Winchester Supreme.
For those who never liked homework.

Figure 16–1
Courtesy of TBWA Kerlick Switzer

But love field trips.

 Winchester has done your homework for you. About a decade's worth.
Developing a new line of ammunition
that matches the performance of the
best handloads.

We call it Supreme.° And there's a
hand-loading, benchrest-shooting
bunch of writers out there that wouldn't
dispute the name. Not after testing it
against their own pet loads.

Supreme starts with the bullet hand-
loaders wish they could start with
Winchester's Silvertip° Boattail. Designed with sophisticated aero-ballistics
computer programs, the bullet has the
best combination yet of accuracy, down-
range energy and knockdown power.

With our Silvertips, and a couple
of great Hornadys,° we're manufacturing
Supreme cartridges to handload specs,
slowing down production, quadrupling
quality control, and hand-inspecting
every round.

Such perfection doesn't come cheap.
Nor in any great quantity. Nor in any
but the most popular cartridges for now.
But if you do get your hands on a box,
you won't need to handload to find
the perfect round.
You'll just have to find
the perfect trophy to
use it on.

And you still get the highest marks in the class.

". . . the trip came down to an afternoon
at the range to shoot Supreme. What com-
menced was an unmatched exhibition of
consistent accuracy from factory-loaded
ammunition. Up and down the line groups
in the one-inch range were commonplace.
Some sub-one-inch groups were turned in,
too!"   *Bill Miller, North American Hunter.*

"We got 3 shots in a half-inch with handloads built for the rifle before I left home.
We got 5 shots in .89-inch here. So it shot
just as good as our handloads did."
Hal Swigget, Harris Publications

". . . I got two five-shot groups from (a)
Mannlicher, using the 180-grain Supreme
Silvertip ammunition, which duplicated the
results I expect with the handload."
Jim Fender, Guns Magazine

"In two different .243's the Supreme's
100-grain soft-point boattail ammo shot
5-shot groups under one inch at 100 yards . . .
The 5-shot average with (a KDF .30-06) was
one inch, and numerous 3-shot groups were
half that."   *Dave Hetzler, Petersen's Hunting*

"I fired a five-shot string with a .22-250
using the new Supreme ammunition which
measured .65-inch."

"The bottom line is that Winchester
Supreme ammo is loaded with great care,
and the results show up on target."
Rick Jamison, Shooting Times

Figure 16–1 (continued)

readers to take the next step. That means not only asking for the order but remembering to include important ordering details such as:

- The company's name and address
- Toll-free phone or local TELEX and FAX numbers
- Directions, prices, store hours, and branch locations
- A list of distributors, dealers, or sales reps (if applicable)
- Exact instruction for placing orders, including credit terms
- Guarantee and warranty information
- Shipping and service terms.

Get Your Facts Straight

In *The Copywriter's Handbook,* Bob Bly recommends that you follow one of the following two outlines in gathering information to write a product or service brochure.

Product Brochure Outline

    I. INTRODUCTION—a capsule description of what the product is and why the readers should be interested in it.

    II. BENEFITS—a list of the major reasons people should buy the product.

   III. FEATURES—highlights of the important features that make the product superior to its competition or are particularly well suited to the prospects' needs.

   IV. METHOD OF OPERATION

      A. Overview of how the product works

      B. Results of lab tests and other tests that demonstrate and prove the product's superior performance

    V. APPLICATIONS—and uses of the product.

Figure 16–2
Courtesy of TBWA Kerlick Switzer

Figure 16–2 (continued)

Figure 16–2 (continued)

Figure 16–2 (continued)

Our homes. Our families. Our futures. Everything.

When U.S.G. put its Metals division on the auctioneer's block, we saw how life in Pinckneyville, Illinois could change drastically. Another company could buy us out and take the whole operation elsewhere. Leaving much of the town's workforce without jobs. And seriously affecting the lives of all 3,300 residents of Pinckneyville.

We didn't see why that should happen when we had a product so good it commands 85% of the market.

So we banded together, many of us mortgaging everything we had, and putting our careers and families' futures on the line, we bought the company. We named it GS Metals. And through the entire transition to self-ownership, we haven't missed a beat. The same people who made Grip Strut the number one product on the market are leading GS Metals today, ensuring the quality of Grip Strut, Globe Strut, and Globetray. And though our customers will tell you we delivered great products and services in the past, we clearly have more incentive than ever to stay on top.

So now everyone, especially our customers, can rest easy. Our operations are intact. Our sales are strong. Our company's future is secure.

And so is Josh's, Johnathon's, Jerad's, and Amy's.

Figure 16–2 (continued)

VI. PRODUCT AVAILABILITY

    A. Models

    B. Sizes

    C. Materials

    D. Colors

    E. Options

    F. Accessories

VII. SELECTION GUIDE—charts, graphs, and other information designed to help the readers select the model or version that best meets their needs.

VIII. PRICES

    A. Pricing for current models

    B. Quantity discounts available

    C. Shipping and handling information

Most manufacturers prefer to put pricing information on a separate sheet so as not to date the brochure.

IX. TECHNICAL SPECIFICATIONS—such as electrical requirements, power consumption, safety inspections, temperature range, proper operating conditions, resistance to moisture, cleaning methods, storage conditions, chemical properties, compatibility with other devices, and other characteristics and limitations of the product.

X. COMPANY BACKGROUND—this section is designed to show that the product is made by a solid, reputable organization that stands behind its products.

XI. PRODUCT SUPPORT AND SERVICE

    A. Toll-free hotlines and other telephone assistance

    B. Installation

    C. Training available

    D. Service and repair policies

    E. Maintenance programs

    F. Warranty and guarantee information

XII. HOW TO ORDER

    A. Ordering instructions

    B. Credit cards accepted

    C. How to get more information or answers to questions

    D. Locations of sales reps or distributor outlets

Service Brochure Outline

I. INTRODUCTION

    A. Capsule summary or brief list of services offered

    B. Type of clients handled

    C. Statement of firm's philosophy

    D. Reasons the readers should consider hiring the firm

II. SERVICES OFFERED—detailed description of the various services offered by the firm and how they satisfy client needs.

III. BENEFITS— discussion of what the readers will gain from the service and why they should hire the firm instead of the competition.

IV. BACKGROUND INFORMATION—this section (optional) examines the problems the service is designed to solve and offers free advice on how to evaluate the problem and select professional help. Such free information, although not a direct sales pitch, adds to the value of the brochure and encourages the readers to keep the literature instead of tossing it into "the circular file."

V. METHODOLOGY—an outline of the firm's method of doing business with clients.

VI. CLIENT LIST—a partial list of well-known people or

organizations who are satisfied users of the firm's services.

VII. TESTIMONIALS—endorsements from satisfied clients. Presented as short quotations written in the client's own words and attributed to a specific person.

VIII. FEES AND TERMS—describes the fees for each service, terms, and any guarantees made by the firm.

IX. BIOGRAPHICAL INFORMATION—capsule biographies highlighting the credentials of the key employees plus an overall capsule biography of the firm.

X. THE NEXT STEP—instructions on what the readers should do next if interested in hiring the firm or learning more about a specific service.

Whether you're writing a product brochure or a service brochure, once you've got your information together, make sure you have a clear idea of which way to go by taking a moment to answer the following questions:

1. What is the subject of the brochure?

2. What is the purpose of this brochure?

3. Who is the audience?

4. Which products (or services) will be featured in the brochure?

5. How will the brochure be used and distributed?

6. Do I already know everything I have to know about this product or is additional research required?

7. Is there a rough layout, outline, or other description of the proposed brochure?

8. What is the budget for the brochure?

9. What photos and illustrations should be used?

10. What size will the brochure be?

11. What length will it be—approximately how many pages?

Five Easy Steps to Writing a Brochure

You're probably overwhelmed by a lot of information right now. So where do you start? Here's a quick and painless way to get your feet wet:

1. *Organize your selling points* into a logical sequence that provides all the information readers need to take the desired action. You may find it easier to think in terms of a headline, body copy, and closing arguments—or a beginning, middle, and end.

2. *Mentally divide your brochure* into short, easy-to-read sections.

3. *Then write fully descriptive headings and subheads.* Some people will only skim a brochure and you don't want them to miss the main selling message.

4. *Start "filling in the blanks."* Tell a story and weave in the benefits, features, and facts that will excite the readers about your product or service.

5. *Never leave your readers hanging.* Ask for the order and always tell them what to do next.

EXERCISE •

Dancing the Brochure Boogie

You're the marketing director of the Moo Town National Bank and the bank wants to begin loaning out money to high school seniors for college tuition. What graphic, headline, and subhead would you use on the front cover of your promotional brochure to announce this program?

My Cover Graphic Idea Is

_____

_____

_____

My Cover Headline Idea Is

_____

_____

_____

_____

My Optional Cover Subhead Idea Is

_____

_____

_____

_____

Helpful Hint: Remember, creativity isn't the key here . . . communication is. So don't be afraid to use tried and true images that say "college" to high school seniors. Images such as graduation caps, diplomas, and lots of little dollar signs are a good start. There's a reason everyone uses them—they work!

17.

....

Take the Direct Approach with Direct Mail

Direct response advertising (also known as direct marketing) is any type of advertising that asks someone to take action now—right this minute. That action can be mailing back a reply card, sending in a payment, phoning an 800 number, renewing a subscription or a membership, clipping a coupon, becoming a donor, or entering a sweepstakes. But direct response advertising has to create immediate action rather than simply contributing to general awareness as many other types of advertising do.

The difference between a direct response ad or mailing and a nondirect response ad or mailing is that with direct response the results are immediately measurable. You know right away whether your advertising has hit or missed.

That's probably why so much direct response advertising is tested in small quantities before it rolls out to a larger audience. It's much better to fail with a small project than to take a major (and expensive) nose dive directly into cement.

There are five different forms of direct response advertising:

1. Direct mail

2. Direct response print ads (usually found in newspapers or magazines)

3. Direct response TV or radio spots

4. Direct response telephone calls (called telemarketing)

5. Direct response flyers and brochures

Direct mail is the hardest form to master because all of the elements (or pieces) have to work together to make the sale. There are several types of direct mail you may be called upon to write:

- *A multi-element letter package* (Figure 17–1) consists of an outer envelope, a letter, a reply device (such as a business reply postcard or form), and usually one or more explanatory inserts such as a brochure.

|||||| CyberTel

CyberTel Cellular Telephone Company
1935 Beltway Drive
St. Louis, MO 63114

An exclusive invitation for:

Sample A. Sample
1234 Sample Dr.
Anytown, US   XXXXX

A Unique Cellular Phone
Opportunity inside...

Outer envelope

Figure 17–1
Courtesy of Shoss and Associates

IIIII CyberTel

CyberTel Cellular Telephone Company

Dear Sample A. Sample:

As a person with proven business and personal success, you have been selected to receive a very unique offer available only to an exclusive few in the St. Louis area.

We'd like to put a CyberTel Cellular Phone in your car--at our expense--for 60 days. We want you to see for yourself just how much more productive you can be when you eliminate drive time waste.

You alone know how valuable your time is, and how much of it is unavoidably wasted by the time you have to spend in your car.

> Consider the number of decisions that are put on hold until you can get back to the office.

> The number of times you've returned to the office only to get back in your car to return to a client or make a hastily-called meeting.

> Or how often you've been on your way to an appointment at the very time your client is calling to cancel.

> Consider, too, the times your colleagues or family have been waiting to hear from you when you've been out of reach in your car.

Doesn't it make sense to take advantage of the time and dollar savings a cellular phone offers? Now, for a limited time, you may discover for yourself how turning drive time into prime time can recapture hours that are routinely lost forever. Time that could change your productivity and your bottom line profits.

You deserve a cellular phone. Not because it's a status symbol. Not because it make you look good. But because a phone in your car will help you be better at what you already do so well. Successful people share many traits--confidence, intelligence, ingenuity--and making the most use of all their time. Whether it's business or personal time you're saving, it's irretrievable once

Letter

Figure 17–1 (continued)

NO POSTAGE
NECESSARY
IF MAILED
IN THE
UNITED STATES

BUSINESS REPLY MAIL
FIRST CLASS PERMIT NO. 8405 ST. LOUIS, MO

POSTAGE WILL BE PAID BY ADDRESSEE

CyberTel Cellular Telephone Company
1935 Beltway Drive
St. Louis, MO 63114-9913

Attention: Jayne Aydt

Reply card

Consider the facts...
A CyberTel Cellular Phone means a more productive business and personal life

- An average of 10 working hours a week are lost by a business person in travel time during the business day. A total of 12 weeks every year.
- Waiting for "call time" is a thing of the past. Cellular systems today can handle 50,000 calls an hour.
- By 1990, more than 2.5 million people will be using cellular mobile telephones.

Cost of Out-Of-Touch Time
Drive Time's Lost Productivity . . . based on 8-hour day, 255 working days per year

Annual Salary	1 Hour Per Day Annualized	2 Hours Per Day Annualized	3 Hours Per Day Annualized	CyberTel Phone Lease/Usage Annualized
$ 25,000	$ 3,125.00	$ 6,250.00	$ 9,375.00	$ 749.40
$ 35,000	$ 4,375.00	$ 8,750.00	$13,250.00	$ 749.40
$ 45,000	$ 5,625.00	$11,250.00	$16,875.00	$ 749.40
$ 50,000	$ 6,250.00	$12,500.00	$18,750.00	$ 749.40
$ 75,000	$ 9,375.00	$18,750.00	$28,125.00	$ 749.40
$100,000	$12,500.00	$25,000.00	$37,500.00	$ 749.40

Does not include FICA taxes @ 7.05% or fringe benefits.

Rental of $19.95 per month over 12-month period	$ 239.40
Usage of 125 minutes per month for 12-month period	$ 510.00
	$ 749.40

© CyberTel 1989

Rate card

Figure 17–1 (continued)

- A *self-mailer* (Figure 17–2) is a less expensive, all-in-one-piece mailing that doesn't need an outer envelope. (Usually a self-mailer is stapled or sealed shut before being mailed.)

- A *multicoupon mailer* (Figure 17–3) is an outer envelope containing many different coupons and offers that sometimes includes a personal letter and a reply device.

- A *catalog* (Figure 17–4) is a descriptive offering of one or more items that may or may not contain a letter but almost always contains a reply device.

The multi-element package is probably the most challenging type of direct mail, since you're usually dealing with at least three pieces:

1. The outer envelope

2. The letter

3. The reply device

Most of the time, a brief supplementary brochure is also included.

Although the letter is the heart of any direct mail package and the outer envelope has to be considered carefully, every piece must carry its own weight.

In 65 percent of mail packages, *the letter sold the item,* while the brochure made the sale 25 percent of the time. The reply device only sold the item 10 percent of the time, but it was still important because capturing responses (and names for future mailings) is essential to the success of many direct mail programs.

It's a lot easier to begin writing a direct mail multi-element package if you think of it as a personal sales call:

- The *envelope* is what gets the prospect to open the door.

- The *letter* is the person-to-person communication—the chatty, one-on-one conversation about the product or service that goes on once the door gets opened.

- The *brochure* assumes a more formal tone in explaining the offer further and lending additional support.

Figure 17–2
Courtesy of Shoss and Associates

Figure 17–3
Courtesy of Shoss and Associates

Figure 17–3
(continued)

CITICORP◆DINERS CLUB CARTE BLANCHE

Dear Cardmember:

It is a pleasure to present this beautiful collection of fashionable furs for you to wear or give as a luxurious gift.

Each garment is formed of soft, thick pelts which have been painstakingly matched for color, size and length of hair. And each fur is accompanied by a Certificate of Appraisal to confirm its value, as well as a Fur Care Guide to help you maintain its beauty.

Of course as a valued Cardmember, you can charge your selection to your Diners Club or Carte Blanche account . . . and enjoy the convenience of monthly installments with no down payment and no finance charge.

Because we believe you should not make an important purchase such as this without first trying on your choice of furs, we urge you to take advantage of the no risk evaluation period.

Here is your opportunity to actually experience the beauty of these furs. If you're not completely delighted with your choice, you may return it within 30 days and receive full credit for any payments made.

To order simply complete the Evaluation Certificate and mail—or for faster service, call the toll-free number.

Cordially,

Mark L. Walker

Mark L. Walker
Senior Vice President

Citicorp Diners Club Inc. is the service agent for Citibank (South Dakota), N.A., issuer of the Diners Club Card.

The final touch . . .

Crowning glory in a Mink Beret

For head to toe perfection. Gleaming mink beret adds a marvelous flair to the Mink Coat, an elegant contrast for your cloth coat or jacket.

Natural Ranch Mink

Beret, one size

fits all.

Fur origin:
USA or Denmark

*Natural Ranch Mink Beret (Item #018)
$398.90* or $38.90 a month* for 10 months.*

A halo of shimmering Blue Fox

Exquisite full-skin hat is an elegant complement to the Blue Fox Jacket or Coat. Brightener-added, one-size hat features a pale grey knitted crown. Warm and luxurious . . . it gives a perfect finished look.

Fur origin:
Finland or Norway

*Blue Fox Hat (Item #017)
$179.90* or $35.98 a month* for 5 months.*

See order form for details

Personalized with your monogram

Your fur creation will proudly display your initials in graceful script letters on a ribbon label sewn into the garment.

Beautifully delivered

Your fur will arrive in a specially designed gift box which will include a contoured fur hanger, Fur Care Guide, and Certificate of Appraisal.

MOISTEN HERE

CITICORP◆DINERS CLUB CARTE BLANCHE

30-DAY NO RISK† EVALUATION

YES! Please send me the merchandise indicated below to examine for 30 days risk-free†. I understand that I will be billed after you have shipped my total order. I may return the merchandise anytime within 30 days and receive full credit for any payments I have made. Please charge my Diners Club or Carte Blanche account according to the terms I have checked below.

THERE IS NO FINANCE CHARGE AND NO DOWN PAYMENT

† ALL ORDERS ARE SUBJECT TO CREDIT APPROVAL

Please check payment plan desired
☐ Single Payment Plan†   ☐ Monthly Payment Plan

Qty	Description	Size 6-20	Height	Weight	Dress Size	MONOGRAM Members Name from first to last	Single Payment Plan†	Equal Monthly Payments*	Shipping Handling & Insurance*
	Blue Fox Jacket (Item #010)						$ 995.00	20 @ $ 49.75	$12.95
	Reversible Opossum Coat (Item #011)						$ 995.00	20 @ $ 49.75	$12.95
	Ranch Mink Coat (Item #012)						$2995.00	25 @ $119.80	$14.95
	Blue Fox Coat (Item #013)						$1995.00	25 @ $ 79.80	$14.95
	Spotted Fox Coat (Item #014)						$2995.00	25 @ $119.80	$14.95
	Crystal Fox Jacket (Item #015)						$2495.00	25 @ $ 99.80	$14.95
	Natural Pastel Mink and Fox Jacket (Item #016)						$1495.00	25 @ $ 59.80	$12.95
	Blue Fox Hat (Item #017)						$ 179.90	5 @ $ 35.98	$ 7.95
	Natural Ranch Mink Beret (Item #018)						$ 349.90	10 @ $ 34.99	$ 7.95

Shipping, handling and insurance charge as indicated above plus applicable Illinois sales tax will be added to the first installment for the Monthly Payment Plan or to the Single Payment Plan. Offer is valid for 120 days after receipt. Please allow three (3) to four (4) weeks for delivery.

THERE IS NO FINANCE CHARGE AND NO DOWN PAYMENT. The total amount of payments (total sales price) under the Monthly Payment Plan is equal to the Single Payment Plan price. If the Cardmember fails to pay any portion of the total payments due, the entire unpaid balance shall at Diners Club or Carte Blanche election, become immediately due.

†Amount equals cash down.

PHONE TOLL-FREE: 1-800-621-1203 Monday-Friday 24 hours, Saturday & Sunday 7 AM to 7 PM Central Time. This number is for ordering merchandise or for questions about merchandise only. Please have this form and your Diners Club or Carte Blanche card at hand when you call.

MANUFACTURER'S LIMITED WARRANTY. Warranty information will be sent to you with the merchandise, or for a free copy now, write Diners Club/Carte Blanche Members Department, P.O. Box 9057, Des Plaines, IL 60017-9370. Please specify product name and item number.

My Diners Club or Carte Blanche Account Number is:

Valid from: _____   Thru: _____

(Order must be signed to be valid)

Member's Name _____

Member's Signature _____

(required to process your order)

If your label has a Post Office Box or, if you wish to have your merchandise shipped to a different address, please indicate below.

SHIP TO:

Name (print) _____

Address _____ (cannot be shipped to a P.O. box)

City/State/Zip _____

Phone (area code) _____ (required to process the order)

Hamet, Inc. is the seller of the goods.

146/727-710/02

REMOVE PEEL OFF LABEL FROM BACK COVER AND AFFIX HERE WHETHER ADDRESS IS CORRECT OR NOT

▼ Detach here ▼

Detach here, fold over, moisten and mail back postage-free

- The optional *lift letter* (also called a publisher's note) provides another reason to take action. This brief note is usually from someone other than the person writing the primary letter.

- The *reply device* asks for a commitment once the "sale" is made—the step that the respondent has to take for the mailing to be considered a success.

Figure 17–4
Courtesy of The Spice Merchant

Teaser Tactics

Since most direct mail ends up in the wastebasket, the first challenge of any multi-element direct mail piece is to get the recipient to open the outside envelope.

In many cases, as when you are mailing to an existing customer or present donor, you may decide that the best tactic is not to have any copy on the outer envelope at all, but instead to simply use the sender's logo and return address in the upper left-hand corner (called a *corner card*). In other mailings, a classy offer or a company's image may require using a discreet, nonpromotional line of copy such as: "Inside . . . an important offer exclusively for you." or "Your invitation is enclosed."

When you feel the tone of the mailing should be more promotional, your envelope copy can include a teaser line, the promise of a benefit, or a deliciously half-told tale. An example of the latter: "I was coming out of a cloud bank when suddenly my instruments failed . . ." (for a set of professional pilot's maps), or "Fall under the spell of Mexican magic tonight and save $4!" (for a restaurant promotion).

Another way to tease a recipient is to provide an enticing glimpse inside your envelope and (hopefully) increase the odds your mailing will be read.

Here are some good bets for teaser items to reveal through one or more of the windows in your envelope:

1. An enthusiastic testimonial, or better yet, a photo with a catchy quote.

2. A sample of your product, e.g., "The FREE Executive Guide to Personal Fortune."

3. Tokens that can be cashed in by returning the response card.

4. An intriguing picture.

5. A decal or bumper sticker.

6. A peel-and-stick label.

7. A special stamp.

8. A simulated check—everybody likes to open an envelope if it looks like there's a check inside.

EXERCISE ••••••••••••••••••••••••••••••••••

Dummy Smarts

The easiest way to start writing a multi-element package is to create a "dummy"—a paper model of what you think your package will eventually look like. The dummy doesn't have to be fancy or artistic; right now it's just a helpful starting point for your writing.

Use what you already know about writing teasers for direct mail—and headlines for ads—to complete this exercise. What follows is a dummy for a standard direct mail package that includes an outer mailing envelope, a one-page, one-sided letter, and a reply device. In this case, the reply device is a postcard with postage that is prepaid by the business that hopes to get it back—called a business reply card or BRC.

Think of how you'd sell a cheesecake-of-the-month club to hungry consumers as you smarten up the following dummy.

Outer envelope

Standard size letter—8½×10

Postcard-size business reply card (BRC)

Now sit back, relax, and think of:

1. A teaser line for your outer envelope

_____

_____

2. A headline for your letter that contains the number-one benefit

_____

_____

3. An opening paragraph for your letter (11 words or less) that will grab your readers' attention

_____

_____

_____

_____

_____

_____

4. A closing paragraph that contains a strong call to action

_____

_____

_____

_____

_____

_____

_____

_____

_____

As you do this exercise, remember that your mailing package will have to flow in a natural progression from what you say on the envelope to what you say in your letter. Your message should also continue naturally through the brochure and the reply device. Remember . . .

- The *envelope* must be persuasive enough to pull your readers in and make them want to look inside.

- The *letter* must discuss the readers' needs, product benefits, features, and how to respond. It should always contain a postscript that either restates the major benefit or gives the recipients another good reason to respond now.

- The *reply device* must not only encourage responding now but must restate the entire offer. Why? Because many times the reply card is the only thing readers keep—long after the other materials have been thrown away, along with all your dazzling selling points. Be sure to repeat the benefits and essentials of the offer on the reply device and in the brochure, if you're including one.

Once you've worked out a dummy for your direct mail pieces, you're ready to go back and fill in the blanks.

Here's a handy list of questions you can use to double-check the effectiveness of your direct mail pieces (and direct response ads):

1. Does the outside envelope and letter opening capture the reader's attention?

2. Does the copy seem to really "speak" to you?

3. Do the voice, style, and vocabulary represent the product accurately?

4. Will anything—a word, phrase, idea, or visual element— cause the reader to slow down (or stop cold) before the postscript?

5. Does the copy sound knowledgeable . . . in plain English?

6. Does the copy create vivid images about how the product or service works, smells, tastes, feels, and looks . . . or how it helps the prospect work, feel, or look?

7. Does the copy address all of the concerns of your audience or audiences?

8. Are the arguments believable or too good to be true?

9. Do you know exactly what to do to take action? And how and where and when to do it?

10. Does the copy ask for the order frequently?

11. Does it present the selling message in a sentence or two?

12. Do you know clearly what you'll miss by not responding now?

Inviting Graphics in Direct Mail

Now that you've spent effort and creative energy coming up with some half-decent direct response copy, remember to make it easy to read visually as well. If the letter looks complicated or complex or time-consuming, it may turn off your reader.

To make your letter easier to read, try these graphic tips for more visual appeal:

1. *Use short paragraphs.* Write six or seven lines at most.

2. *Use wide margins.* Allow an inch and a half on each side.

3. *Underline words for emphasis.* But don't overdo it.

4. *Pick an appropriate color of paper for your particular audience.* If you run a beauty shop, use pink, yellow, or lavender. If you're aiming at businesspeople, use white, off-white, or maybe gray.

5. *Don't make letters too short.* Two to four pages is best. Remember, if someone is interested in your proposition, he or she will take the time to read a fairly long letter. A short letter just can't provide enough space to tell your story ... and your prospect will recognize this.

6. *Use a postscript at the end of your letter.* It is probably the most read part of the letter. Use it to restate your major benefit, offer some incentive, or ask the prospect to respond in some specific way.

7. *Use a good quality typewriter, quality printer, or laser printer.*

8. To give your letter instant readability, *use white space whenever possible.* You can do this by listing information in column form using numbers, asterisks, or bullets.

9. *Use headlines throughout your letter.* They help the reader's eye and the prospect can skip to the exact paragraph of interest quickly and easily.

18.

· ·

Lights! Camera! TV!

Believe it or not, you now have a strong enough grounding in the fundamentals to write a TV commercial. You'll go through the same basic thinking and fact-finding steps that you used in print. But this time, instead of creating a headline, support claims, closing arguments, and call to action, you'll hammer out a beginning, middle, and end—a kind of minidrama told in highly visual terms.

After all, TV is a medium of pictures not words. You have to make your pictures tell the story, and what you show is more important than what you say. Sight and sound have to work together closely and, in fact, words usually take a back seat. They're strictly there to explain what the pictures are showing.

In writing a TV commercial, you have to be sure your pictures really deliver one main selling message. So if your sales pitch requires a lot of words, remember to keep the pictures simple. And if you're using complex graphics, keep the words to a minimum.

Backward Flips

As with all advertising, the hardest part of writing TV commercials is knowing where to begin. Here are some quick tips to get you started:

1. *Think of the end of the commercial first and start there.* What final impression do you want to leave with your viewers? A great ending is the first step toward a great beginning.

2. *Now, thinking in purely visual terms, work backwards and decide what it is you want to accomplish.* Weave in your supporting claims and ideas. Build. Elaborate.

3. *Finally, concentrate on your opening and think of a strong, simple selling idea.* People aren't paying attention to your commercial, so you have to create a grabber opening that conveys the central idea and captures immediate interest.

Once you've started to rough out a beginning, middle, and end, go back and take a closer look at each of these three sections.

The Beginning (or Opening)

This section should open the window for the viewer and provide important information about what's going on. Whether it is to establish a scene, introduce the characters, or dramatize the problem, you must begin your commercial in a way that makes it easy for people to get into it immediately.

Some common beginning section problems include:

1. *Too many words.* The openings of many commercials are overwritten. A wordy or overelaborate opening creates time problems and makes the rest of the commercial sound rushed. Tell the viewers what you're going to tell them, but do it quickly.

2. *Lack of a clear message.* Many commercials suffer from vague openings. In many cases, this happens because the writer was trying too hard to be clever and original. Unfortunately, something that may take a long time to think up may also take a long time for the viewer to understand. Tricky visuals or word play usually result in confusion instead of interest. So tell the viewers what you're going to tell them *clearly.*

3. *Lack of interest.* This happens when there are dull words and graphics, and when the main selling message is not benefit-oriented. If you bore viewers, they'll vote "no" with their remote control units.

The Middle

In the middle section it's especially important to be clear and say what you mean—meaningfully, memorably, and rhythmically.

The basic question you must answer in the middle of your commercial is, "What proof is needed here for people to believe what you're promising?" Sometimes all you have to do is write convincing "reason-why" copy or stage a dramatic demonstration using strong visuals. And sometimes it's unbelievably tough because the product has no dramatic difference, or it's low interest, or the benefits are really hard to visualize. Whether it's easy or tough, your middle section has got to deliver the goods.

The End

And finally, take another look at your fond farewell. In addition to providing the necessary information, the end of your commercial should reward the viewer. Whether it's a clever phrase, a memorable musical finish, a sentimental tug at the heart, or the perfect punch line, you must tie together your commercial visually *and* verbally.

More Things to Remember About TV

- To keep your budget reasonable, try not to use special effects, jingles, actors, animation, computer graphics, or location shooting, since these can shoot the cost of a TV commercial sky high.

- Get straight to the point. In a 60-second commercial you have a maximum of 90 words to make your case; in a 30-

second commercial, you have half of that. Keep selling every second you're on the air.

- If you are selling a product that can be purchased off the shelf, show the label. Use close-ups to draw attention to the package. People will buy the product if they remember it from your commercial.

- Show motion. Show cars driving, maple syrup pouring, airplanes flying, popcorn popping, soda fizzing. Keep it moving.

- Repeat the product name and the main selling point at least twice so viewers remember what you're selling. It's also possible that many viewers were daydreaming during the beginning of your spot, so be sure by the end they know who you are and what you're trying to get them to do.

- Avoid cliché situations that may bore viewers. Try to make your commercials fresh, memorable, and a little bit different. Sometimes this can be accomplished through offbeat casting.

- In local retail commercials, give the address and clear directions to the store. If the store has many locations, urge viewers to consult their phone books for the location nearest them.

Bob Bly's 12 Types of TV Commercials

If you've read this far, you know that Bob Bly loves to number things. Here is Bob's list of the 12 most common types of TV commercials:

1. *Demonstrations* show how a product works. There are actually several types of demo ads:

   - *The side-by-side demo* compares your product with another.

   - *The before-and-after demo* dramatizes the benefit and the problem.

- *The performance demo* dramatizes how well your product works.

- *The in-use demo* actually shows people new ways to use the product (e.g., a recipe or a serving idea).

Demos can be real or they can be symbolic. For example, a commercial can be based on the graphic representation of a new product technology. Other effective demos can be based on test results, sales figures, popularity, or uniqueness. If they are honest, demonstrations are generally very effective.

2. *Testimonials* add credibility to a claim. People more readily believe praise for a product when it comes from a customer or a third party rather than from a manufacturer. Testimonials are almost always successful if you make them credible. Celebrities or real people can be effective but avoid irrelevant celebrities whose fame has no natural connection with your product or your customers. Irrelevant celebrities tend to steal attention from your product and they're expensive to boot.

3. *Stand-up presenter.* In this type of commercial, an actor stands before the camera and delivers a straightforward sales pitch on the virtues of the product. It's important to remember to add visual information to the verbal information provided by your talking person.

4. *Slice of life* commercials are miniature plays centering around two or more people and a story involving the product. These are some of the best commercials as well as the worst.

5. *Life-style advertising* focuses on the user and how the product fits into his or her life style. Anheuser-Busch's "This Bud's for you" campaign is a good example.

6. *Animations or cartoons* pull well with children but poorly with adults. They also tend to be very expensive to produce well.

7. *Jingles* are advertising slogans set to music. If catchy, these can catapult a product over its competition.

8. *Visuals as hero* commercials feature the filmmaking not the selling. Does this type of commercial sell products? The jury is still out but they certainly do arouse curiosity. They strongly resemble a visual collage in its approach.

9. *Humor.* Funny commercials have become increasingly popular in recent years.

10. *Continuing characters.* Fictional persons who appear in a series of commercials and print ads. Extremely effective in building brand recognition.

11. *Reason-why copy* lists the reasons people should buy the product. All the reasons people like to eat franks, for instance.

12. *Emotion.* Commercials that use nostalgia, charm, or sentiment to tug at the heartstrings. Hard to write. Most copywriters have a better shot sticking to demonstrations, pitches, testimonials, and other "straight-sell" formats.

The Four Faces of TV

The four basic commercial lengths are 10, 30, 60, and 120 seconds. Ten-second commercials are usually identification spots. They simply drive home a product name and support the campaign's 30- or 60-second spots. Most commercials that build preference for a brand name product are either 30 or 60 seconds long. Mail order advertisers use two-minute (120-second) campaigns because they need to deliver more complete information in order to convince people to respond. After all, "operators are standing by now."

EXERCISE ·····················

Star Car

We'll get to this TV-writing exercise in a minute, but first, a word from our sponsor . . .

:30 Demonstration Spot
Zoo World Pets

VIDEO	AUDIO
Shot of hands working on Christmas list . . . frustrated, scratching out socks, ties, etc. Breaks pencil.	DON'T FRET OVER THAT PERFECT HOLIDAY GIFT . . .
Video Transition to close-up of water, pull back to show beautiful aquarium setup.	TAKE A LITTLE LOVE . . . AND JUST ADD WATER (SOUND EFFECT: BUBBLING WATER.)
Zoo World exterior or logo.	AN AQUARIUM SET FROM ZOO WORLD IS A GIFT OF LOVE . . . A GIFT OF LIFE THAT WILL LAST THROUGHOUT THE YEARS.
Shot showing rows of aquariums and close-ups of colorful fish.	
Shot of sample aquarium package.	OUR HOLIDAY SPECIAL PACKAGES INCLUDE AQUARIUMS FROM 5½ to 300 GALLONS . . .
Transition to colorful aquarium setup.	PLUS THE FISH AND ALL THE EXTRAS. ALL YOU DO IS, "JUST ADD WATER!"
Shot of birds with people.	ZOO WORLD ALSO HAS THE LARGEST SELECTION OF BIRDS IN THE MIDWEST . . .
Shot of small animals.	PLUS A WIDE ARRAY OF SMALL ANIMALS AND REPTILES.
Shot of interior to show how large and clean store is.	ZOO WORLD . . . YOUR "SUPER PET STORE".

Logo with address and phone numbers of each location.   NOW WITH FOUR CONVE-
NIENT LOCATIONS.

Using the demonstration spot for Zoo World as an example, write your own 30-second TV demonstration spot for your favorite luxury automobile.

Time your copy by reading it at a normal pace and adding enough "breathing room" to allow for changing visuals. You can either use a stopwatch or the second hand of your wristwatch.

Remember to give your commercial a beginning, middle, and end and to take maximum advantage of the visual power of a demonstration.

VIDEO   **AUDIO**

_____   _____

_____   _____

_____   _____

_____   _____

_____   _____

_____   _____

_____   _____

_____   _____

_____   _____

_____   _____

_____   _____

_____   _____

_____   _____

_____   _____

_____   _____

_____   _____

_____   _____

_____   _____

_____   _____

_____   _____

_____   _____

_____   _____

_____   _____

_____   _____

_____   _____

_____   _____

_____   _____

Helpful Hint: You're on target if you launch right into the most interesting, exciting, or funny part of the commercial within the first few seconds. Unlike European commercials, which last longer and are often subtle, American commercials have 30 seconds to grab viewers by the throat (or the funny bone) or lose them to the kitchen or the bathroom.

19.

●●●

Tuning in for Radio

Welcome to "The Theater of the Mind." While print advertising appeals to the reader, a radio commercial (known
as a *radio spot*) appeals to the listener and must create an entire
world inside his or her imagination. A radio spot also needs to be
carefully timed so it fits the 60-second time period (sometimes only
30 seconds) that has been purchased from the radio station.

Basically, there are three types of radio commercials: (1) The
straight announcer pitch, (2) the dramatic situation, and (3) the
music and copy combination.

Straight Announcer Pitch

In the straight announcer pitch, an announcer talks directly to the
audience. The two basic tools at your disposal in writing this kind
of spot are the announcer's voice and your own words. You can
add anything you want to make it interesting including background
music or sound effects. Here's an example:

GALESBURG GO KARTS
:60

ANNCR: THERE ARE TWO DRIVERS IN MANY OF US. ONE, THE
        "SAFE" DRIVER . . . WHO ALWAYS OBSERVES THE SPEED

LIMIT AND DRIVES DEFENSIVELY. (SOUND EFFECT OF A SAFE, ORDINARY DRIVER).

THE OTHER IS A SPEED-HUNGRY RACE CAR DRIVER (SOUND EFFECT OF RACE CAR OPENING UP AND REVVING AWAY) YEARNING FOR THE THRILL AND CHALLENGE OF AN OPEN ROAD. THE ONE BORN FOR GALESBURG GO KARTS! DRIVE SAFELY ON THE ROAD AND LET GALESBURG GO KARTS SATISFY THE RACE DRIVER IN YOU . . . WITH THEIR VERY OWN ORIGINAL GET UP AND GO CARTS. UNIQUE TO GALESBURG GO KARTS, THESE MAKE KARTING A REAL CHALLENGE FOR ANYONE OF DRIVING AGE. (MORE SOUND EFFECTS OF RACING ENGINES) RACE YOUR FRIENDS ON A BANKED, LE MANS-STYLE RACE COURSE WHERE THE HIGH-REV EXCITEMENT NEVER STOPS. IT'S ADULT FUN . . . OPEN SEVEN DAYS A WEEK FROM ELEVEN A.M. TO MIDNIGHT. TAKE THE OLD BURNHAM BRIDGE WEST TO THE RIVER BOTTOM ROAD. CROSS OVER TO GALESBURG, THEN IT'S JUST THREE MILES WEST TO HAD- LEY . . . HOME OF GALESBURG GO KARTS. CONVE- NIENTLY LOCATED JUST MINUTES FROM DOWNTOWN AND EASY TO GET TO FROM ANYWHERE. IT'S FRESH, IT'S FAST, IT'S FUN. IT'S GALESBURG GO KARTS . . . FOR THE "OTHER DRIVER" IN YOU!

Here's still another example of a straight announcer spot. This one lacks sound effects, but an enthusiastic announcer could make it a highly "listenable" commercial.

ACE RENTAL CAR
:55 seconds

ANNCR: SURPRISES ARE NO FUN WHEN YOU'RE BUYING A NEW CAR. SO WHY TAKE A CHANCE WHEN YOU CAN GET ONE THAT'S ALREADY PROVEN ITSELF . . . IN WRITING . . . FROM ACE RENTAL CAR! THAT'S RIGHT, YOU CAN SEE THE OFFICIAL SERVICE AND MAINTENANCE RECORD OF EVERY ACE CAR BEFORE YOU BUY. THAT MEANS NO SUR- PRISES. STILL WANT MORE ASSURANCE? THEN TAKE ANY ACE CAR TO YOUR MECHANIC AND LET AN EXPERT LOOK

IT OVER BEFORE YOU BUY. YOU'LL BOTH BE IMPRESSED.
WHY IS ACE SO CONFIDENT? THAT'S NO SURPRISE BE-
CAUSE THEY SELECT ONLY THE FINEST AND MOST RE-
CENT MODELS FROM THEIR RENTAL FLEET, THEN BACK
EACH ONE WITH A 12-MONTH/12 THOUSAND MILE WAR-
RANTY. AND ACE CARS ARE EQUIPPED WITH THE MOST
POPULAR OPTIONS. THE ONLY THING THAT WILL SUR-
PRISE YOU IS THE PRICE . . . FAIR, CLEARLY MARKED, AND
A LOT LESS THAN A COMPARABLE NEW CAR. SO IF YOU
THOUGHT HONESTY, INTEGRITY, AND A FAIR DEAL WERE
A THING OF THE PAST, YOU'RE IN FOR A SURPRISE AT
ACE! LOCATED ON DEAKINS ROAD RIGHT NEXT TO EXIT
44A. PHONE 555-1212.

Dramatic Situation

The dramatic situation is an especially entertaining and effective
way to use radio. You develop an event or a miniature story that
places your product in a particular situation. This situation is often
comedic and limited only by your ability to write with a bit of
dramatic flair. Unique voices, sound effects, and music can help
establish your characters quickly and clearly as in the following
commercial for an elite hair designer:

HENRI PHILLIPE
:60

(SOUND EFFECTS OF A COCKTAIL PARTY IN PROGRESS)

WOMAN TO HERSELF: (OH NO! IT'S THE GEEK WITH THE AL-
    FALFA HAIRCUT!)
GEEK: NICE PARTY, HUH?
WOMAN: I JUST CAME FROM THE HAIR DESIGNER'S MYSELF.
GEEK: HAIR DESIGNER'S, HUH? WELL, IT LOOKS FANTASTIC.
    WHERE DID YOU GO?
WOMAN: HENRI PHILLIPE, OF COURSE. (WHERE DID YOU GO
    . . . QUICKIE CUTS?)
GEEK: I GO TO BERNIE'S BARGAIN BARBER.
WOMAN: REALLY! I'D HAVE NEVER GUESSED.
GEEK: I GET THEIR TWO-FOR-ONE SPECIALS.

WOMAN: HOW NICE! (YEAH, GET YOUR HAIR CUT AND YOUR DOG GROOMED FOR HALF PRICE.)

GEEK: BET YOU DON'T GET ANY TWO-FOR-ONE DEALS AT HENRI PHILLIPE.

WOMAN: NO, THEY DO IT RIGHT THE FIRST TIME.

GEEK: HUH?

WOMAN: THE EXPERIENCED STAFF AT HENRI PHILLIPE ARE MORE THAN JUST HAIR CUTTERS. THEY'RE INTERNATION-ALLY TRAINED HAIR DESIGNERS. THEY TAKE THAT EXTRA TIME TO MAKE SURE MY HAIR LOOKS GOOD ON ME. THAT'S WHAT HENRI PHILLIPE MEANS WHEN THEY SAY "HAIR STYLING FOR DISCRIMINATING LADIES AND GEN-TLEMEN."

GEEK: I THOUGHT ALL HAIR PLACES WERE THE SAME.

WOMAN: (THAT'S OBVIOUS!) GUESS YOU LEARN SOMETHING NEW EVERY DAY.

GEEK: PERSONALLY, I STILL LIKE THE TWO-FOR-ONE SPE-CIALS.

WOMAN: WELL, THERE'S TWO OF US NOW, AND IF YOU GO AWAY THERE'LL ONLY BE ONE. ISN'T THAT SPECIAL!

GEEK: HUH?

ANNCR: HENRI PHILLIPE . . . CREATIVE HAIR DESIGN FOR DIS-CRIMINATING LADIES AND GENTLEMEN. 9035 WEST HAR-BOR DRIVE AND 877 LAKERSHIM. HENRI PHILLIPE.

Music and Copy Combination

Because radio was originally developed for music, a music and copy combination gives your words new dimension. Some of the easiest ways to mix words and music in your spot are to

- Start with music and lead into the pitch.
- Start with the pitch and lead into the music.
- Switch back and forth between the music and the pitch.

Here's an example of a "doughnut" spot that features a copy "hole" wedged in between two musical segments.

BENSINGER FORD
:60

(OPENING :15 OF BENSINGER FORD JINGLE)

ANNCR: HALLOWEEN IS UPON US! BUT THAT'S NOT WHY ALL THE OTHER CAR DEALERS ARE SHAKING IN THEIR BOOTS. BENSINGER FORD IS HACKING HIGH PRICES TO THE BONE, AND MAKING HALLOWEEN A REAL TREAT FOR YOU! HOW ABOUT A BRAND NEW TURBO THUNDERBIRD FOR AS LOW AS 13-9-95! A TAURUS WITH V-6 STARTING AT 11-6-95! GET AN ALL NEW AEROSTAR X-L FROM 10-6-95. CHECK OUT A RANGER SUPER CAR STARTING AT 85-95. JUST A FEW OF THE FANTASTIC DEALS DURING THIS HALLOWEEN EXTRAVAGANZA. STOP BY BENSINGER FORD . . . AND SEE FOR YOURSELF WHY THE OTHER GUYS DON'T STAND A GHOST OF A CHANCE!

(CLOSING :10 OF BENSINGER FORD JINGLE)

TAG: BENSINGER FORD . . . WHERE THERE'S ALWAYS A BETTER DEAL. HIGHWAY 40 AND 270.

At the end of many radio commercials, like the one above, there's often a brief piece of copy called the *tag* that contains the address and information about short-term special offers. Sometimes, you'll hear a spot for a national product with a local tag telling people where to buy the product nearby. For example, a tag for a national floral delivery service might say: "In Minneapolis, order your Mother's Day flowers from The Olive Tree Florist on Olive Boulevard. Just $20 for a dozen roses now through Sunday." Many advertisers rotate their tags according to the special offer available during that week.

EXERCISE •

Sound Advice

Choose one or more of the following sound effects and use it (them) as an inspiration for a 60-second dramatic situation spot selling your product or service—or your favorite microwave snack. Be sure to indicate which characters are talking (if there are more than one). Time your spot to allow all the characters to speak normally, without rushing.

Sound Effects

Popcorn popping	Gunshot
Big Italian wedding	Car breathing its last gasp
Foghorn sounding	Violent storm
Western cattle roundup	Microwave buzzer going off
Sizzling sounds	Telephone ringing
Baby crying	Airplane landing

My Dramatic Situation Radio Spot Idea:

_____

_____

_____

_____

_____

_____

_____

_____

_____

_____

_____

_____

_____

_____

_____

_____

_____

_____

_____

Helpful Hint: If the list of sound effects doesn't inspire you, imagine for a moment that you are blind and are listening to two people talk about your product or service. What sounds or dialogue do you hear? You're on the right track if your copy moves at the same pace as an interesting conversation—building steadily toward a conclusion and then delivering a "big finish."

20.

● ●

Clear Your "Voice"

Whatever type of advertising writing you do, people will only respond to it if it's clear, simple, and easy to understand. The fastest shortcut is to *write the way you talk*. Writing experts call this "conversational tone." When your copy has this person-to-person level—even when it's discussing complex subjects—it has the sound of one friend talking to another. And the result is that more people will listen carefully to what you have to say.

Here are some tips for developing a natural conversational "voice" as you write:

- Use everyday expressions—a sure thing, OK, rip-off, totally awesome.

- Use contractions whenever possible—they're, you're, it's, here's, we've, I'm.

- Use simple words and avoid being a language snob at all costs. Choose the one-dollar word over the five-dollar one. Use "do" instead of "accomplish."

- If you must choose between writing naturally and being grammatically correct, write naturally. Everyone will forgive you except your English teachers. (And they're paid to be unforgiving.)

21.

Some Great Consumer Advertising

Consumer advertising is designed to sell a wide variety of goods and services to, you guessed it, consumers. Consumers are people just like you and me who thought they were perfectly content until consumer advertising aroused their secret desire for the latest, the greatest, THAT ONE THING THEY JUST HAD TO HAVE until THE NEXT THING THEY JUST HAD TO HAVE.

Consumer advertising differs from business-to-business advertising because it's aimed primarily at recreational readers or viewers—people who may be open to your advertising message but who are constantly distracted by everything from their kids arguing to the dog barking. Because it's constantly competing to capture a reader's or viewer's attention, consumer advertising tends to be more entertaining than informative, and filled with creativity rather than with hard facts.

Figures 21–1 to 21–3, ads for the Automobile Club of Missouri, illustrate how three variations on one strong central visual (the tow truck) communicate a variety of sales messages with wit and humor.

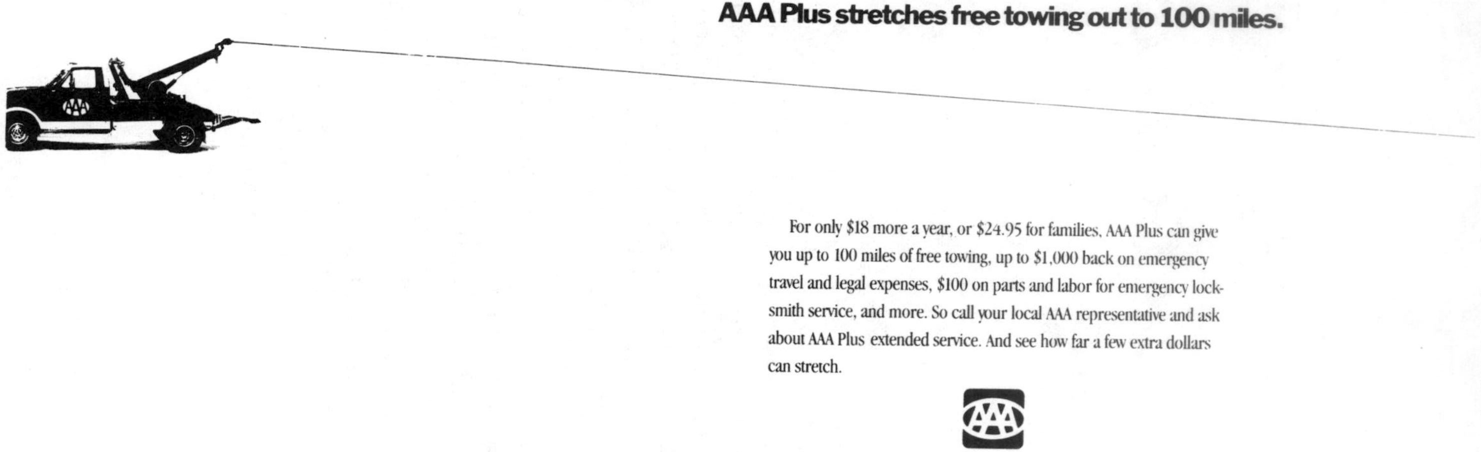

AAA Plus stretches free towing out to 100 miles.

For only $18 more a year, or $24.95 for families, AAA Plus can give you up to 100 miles of free towing, up to $1,000 back on emergency travel and legal expenses, $100 on parts and labor for emergency locksmith service, and more. So call your local AAA representative and ask about AAA Plus extended service. And see how far a few extra dollars can stretch.

Figure 21–1

Courtesy of TBWA Kerlick Switzer. Copyright Automobile Club of Missouri, 1989.

AAA has discounts for cars with anti-theft protection, accident-free drivers, drivers with more than one car, teens who have completed driver's education, mature drivers and more. All on auto insurance that's rated highly by policy-holders for excellent coverage and hassle-free claims service. Call your agent for a fast quote, or send in the attached reply card.

Chances are AAA auto Insurance can lower your premiums.

Auto Insurance

Figure 21–2
Courtesy of TBWA Kerlick Switzer. Copyright Automobile Club of Missouri, 1989.

EXERCISE ••••••••••••••••••••••••••••••••••••

Three Times a Lady

Choose any product aimed at a female consumer. Now think of one central visual that could work with three different headlines for this product. The headlines can be benefit oriented or simply address one interesting aspect of the product. (If you have trouble

Now you can hook up with someone you know for auto financing.

Instead of relying on people you may never see again, you can arrange your financing through someone who'll be there down the road. Your AAA agent. Financing through AAA offers very competitive rates on new and used cars. You can even get pre-approved if you're not quite ready to buy. Finance your next car with someone who'll care about it long after the sale. Call your AAA agent for a fast quote, or clip this coupon for more information.

Figure 21–3

Courtesy of TBWA Kerlick Switzer.

Copyright Automobile Club of Missouri, 1989.

thinking of a product, just pick up any women's, home, or fashion magazine and leaf through the first few pages.)

My Central Visual for These Three Different Product Ads Is:

_____

_____

_____

_____

My Headline for Ad #1 Is:

_____

_____

_____

_____

My Headline for Ad #2 Is:

_____

_____

_____

_____

My Headline for Ad #3 Is:

_____

_____

Helpful Hint: If you have trouble thinking of a central visual that works equally well with three different headlines, start with the headlines first. Make them as effective as possible by choosing the three most important benefits of the product and starting from there. Later, go back to the visual and play around with the possibilities suggested in the headlines. Sure, it's cheating, but it's better than just sitting there!

22.

••

Some Great Business-to-Business Advertising

Business-to-business advertising is sometimes referred to as *trade* or *industrial advertising*, depending on the product or service being pitched. In simple terms, business-to-business advertising is what one company uses to sell products or services to buyers (or decision-makers) at another company.

In the ads shown in Figures 22–1 through 22–3, you can see how benefits are used to make a business reader feel important or knowledgeable—and how the copywriter connects these benefits to becoming a Winchester dealer or buying Vestal's product line.

Generally, business-to-business ads do not ask for the sale but try to generate a lead—to get the businesspeople to raise their hands and say, "Yes, I'm interested." Once the prospect is identified, it's up to the sales force or the follow-up materials to do the real selling.

By and large, business-to-business copy is better off written in short, clear sentences than in complicated, highly sophisticated ones. Try to use simpler words rather than multisyllable ones, and stay away from any buzz words or technical terms that not everyone will understand.

Some ammunition companies could survive without you.

Surprisingly, the largest can't.

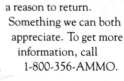 If you don't believe that our doors would close if yours did, you're wrong. No other sporting ammunition manufacturer relies as much upon independent dealers as Winchester.

More than ever, to compete, you need customers coming in and coming back. By merely cutting prices, you may bring them in. But with educational tools to help make them better hunters, you're certain to bring them back. And this year those tools will only be in the hands of Winchester dealers.

They include the new Winchester Success Center™ and Guides to Success™. Specific promotions will also feature valuable educational tools such as our steel shot video, shotshell game guide and CXP™ (Controlled Xpansion Performance) cartridge selector. Our Dream Hunt™ and GMC Sierra truck sweepstakes, as well as our extensive multi-media advertising, refer to these tools and are designed to get customers into the only place where they will be available — a Winchester dealer.

By offering the tools they need for future success, you give your customers a reason to return. Something we can both appreciate. To get more information, call 1-800-356-AMMO.

WINCHESTER®
Because Every Round Counts.™®

Figure 22–1
Courtesy of TBWA Kerlick Switzer

Figure 22-2
Courtesy of Shoss and Associates

Figure 22–3
Courtesy of Shoss and Associates

EXERCISE ••••••••••••••••••••••••••••••

Getting Down to Business

Develop a benefit-oriented headline for the following copy-only, business-to-business ad:

The Body Copy of This "Headless" Ad Reads:

> Engineers who specify Argon products have it pretty easy. No one comes around asking why the valve they chose is leaking. No one has to worry whether the hydrant they specified will work at that crucial moment.
>
> They don't waste time rethinking decisions. Or figuring out where money will come from to cover repairs. They just choose Argon and move on.
>
> Argon products consistently outperform and outlast all others. And our dependability costs less in the long run.
>
> If you want today's choices to look just as good tomorrow, choose Argon the first time.
>
> It's the one answer that makes questions a thing of the past. And lets you keep your free time to yourself.

My Headline Might Be:

_____

_____

_____

_____

Helpful Hint: Fair warning! This exercise is tougher than it looks. But if you start with the relaxed, confident attitude the copywriter tries to create from the first paragraph, you're halfway home. One possibility for an indirect headline: "Easy Does It With Argon."

23.

Some Great Fund-Raising Advertising

The goal of fund raising is to get your prospective or current donor to contribute money to your cause, charity, or organization. To do it well you have to write from your heart as well as your head.

In Figures 23–1 through 23–3, the writer has woven together a rich tapestry of emotions to encourage readers to open their pocketbooks and their wallets.

Notice how the *tone* of each fund-raising solicitation varies depending on the subject of the communication. For the "Disaster-gram" (Figure 23–1), it's short, intense, and dramatic—designed to sound like an urgent telegram. For Ronald McDonald House (Figure 23–2), a temporary haven for families with critically ill children, the tone is warm, intimate, and personal—a message unashamedly written to tug at the heartstrings. And for Rainbow Village (Figure 23–3), a home for retarded children, the tone is just as warm, but more factual—equally balanced between information and sentiment.

The key to writing fund-raising copy is to communicate in simple, powerful terms that create strong images and an even stronger emotional response in your reader.

American Red Cross

DisasterGram

E M E R G E N C Y   D I S P A T C H

DISASTER RELIEF FUND   8:30 AM   7371

YOUR HELP CRITICAL. 185,000 AFRICAN MEN, WOMEN & CHILDREN
STARVING TO DEATH. MOST SEVERE DROUGHT & FAMINE OF CENTURY
CAUSING HOPELESS SITUATION. NO RAIN FOR 2 YEARS. NO CROPS. NO
FOOD. NO WATER.

AMERICAN RED CROSS MUST HELP ELIMINATE DEADLY EPIDEMICS OF
MALNUTRITION AND STARVATION. CAN NOT DO WITHOUT YOU. YOUR GIFT
WILL SAVE LIVES. $4 FEEDS FAMILY OF 4 FOR ONE WEEK. $12 FEEDS
CHILD FOR 3 MONTHS. $48 FOR FULL YEAR.

HELP PICK UP THE TAB. MILLIONS DESPERATELY NEED YOUR HELP.
WITHOUT YOU. . . NOTHING.   WITH YOU, PROMISE OF LIFE FOR
FAMILIES, CHILDREN, IN 12 OF THE MOST RAVAGED OF 27 STARVING
AFRICAN NATIONS.

YOUR GENEROSITY NEVER MORE BADLY NEEDED. WE CAN NOT TURN OUR
BACKS. YOU OFFER ONLY HOPE. PLEASE DETACH CONTRIBUTION CARD
BELOW & RETURN TODAY WITH YOUR GIFT OF LIFE.

THANK YOU

Figure 23–1

Courtesy of American Red Cross, Bi–State Chapter, and Susan Christensen

The Ronald McDonald House
Children's Oncology Services
of Metro St. Louis, Inc.
4381 West Pine
St. Louis, Missouri 63108

"It is a magical house where 4-year-old Shannon 'Bubba' Herron and his family find love and laughter and hope..."

Dear Friend of Ronald McDonald House,

Bubba Herron and the other kids at Ronald McDonald House are different from other kids ... they're stricken with dreaded illnesses like cancer and heart disease ... illnesses too often incurable.

But a year ago I learned that more than 300 of these children and their families have a refuge ... a place where they can stay during medical treatments at St. Louis hospitals ... a place of joy where they can romp with other kids who don't think it's so strange to be bald at age four.

But the magic just begins with the children. For their families "Ronald's House" is a haven of hope and understanding where other parents are going through the same kind of indescribable turmoil ... the heart-wrenching pain of watching their precious children suffer. Where they can share their hopes and their darkest fears, discuss their financial strains; learn to cope with the stress on their families.

But most importantly, it's a place where they can receive comfort and courage and faith which transfers directly to their children, giving them the strength to fight their excruciating battles.

And all of this "magic" is possible only because of contributions like yours and mine. I realize that you receive many charitable requests at this time of year. But no other organization could have a stronger reason for needing your support. To run and staff Ronald McDonald House is fiendishly expensive -- but then magic never does come cheap.

Operating this "house that love built" costs approximately $27 per day per child. If you could find it in your heart to help a little one for just one day ... or, if you can ... two days, three days, maybe even a week or more, you can be part of the magic, too.

Your dollars can maintain and further this magnificent act of faith, this truly helping hand to little children ravaged with nature's most horrible diseases.

For Bubba, and for Mickey, age 5, and for Pammy, age 7, and for Sally, age 3, and for hundreds like them, write your check to Ronald McDonald House and keep the magic happening! For your convenience I've enclosed a reply envelope.

Figure 23-2
Courtesy of Ronald McDonald House and Susan Christensen

143

Thanks so much for your support. During this season of love and togetherness, please join my family in making this a "magical" holiday for Bubba and all the other children at Ronald's House.

Warmest regards,

Bob Forsch

Bob Forsch, Chairman
Ken Boyer Memorial Fund

P.S. You're invited to our Holiday Open House, an old-fashioned get-together with house tours and complimentary refreshments, Dec. 21 & 22, 1:00 to 5:00 P.M.

Figure 23–2 (continued)

EXERCISE ······································

Fun in Fund Raising

Fund-raising Power Words

You	Sharing
Please	Show
Urgent	Only
Help	Grateful
Now	Victim
Thank you	Reach out
Together	Difference
Need	Donation
Voice	Can't Wait
Answer	Generous
Caring	Special

Use some of these fund-raising power words to help you write the headline and opening paragraph for a letter that will raise money for Aid to Victims of Crime, an organization that provides legal, psychological, and financial assistance to crime victims.

Retarded children become adults, too ...

Rainbow Village has found a better answer for the mentally retarded than a lifetime in an institution. The St. Louis area has approximately 60,000 mentally retarded ... all but a small percentage can gain some measure of independence if given help.

A group to belong to, close personal friends, outlets for energies, a job to go to, money to spend and identity are as essential to the self-respect of the retarded adult as to any other. Rainbow Village is a non-institutional facility in St. Louis for the mentally retarded ... some live here, others work, play and continue their education here ... for as long as they can participate or benefit.

Help us continue to provide a better answer. Retarded children become adults, too ...

If you'd like more information, write or call: Rainbow Village, 1240 Dautel Lane, St. Louis, Mo. 63141 (314) 569-2211

RAINBOW VILLAGE 1240 Dautel Lane, St. Louis, MO 63141 (314) 569 2211

Figure 23–3
Courtesy of Shoss and Associates and Susan Christensen

My Headline (Optional):

_____

_____

_____

My Opening Paragraph:

_____

_____

_____

_____

_____

_____

Helpful Hint: Most people who donate to charities are women over age 50. Your heart's in the right place if you imagine yourself writing warmly, personally, and caringly to this typical woman donor and asking for her help—almost as if you're chatting while having a cup of coffee together.

24.

Some Great Financial Advertising

Financial advertising in the past decade has undergone a major creative revolution. Most financial institutions—especially banks, savings and loans, and brokerages—have traditionally promoted their products, rates, and services using an approach perfected at the Joe Friday School of Advertising: "Just the facts, ma'am." They reasoned that most people don't want to be entertained by financial advertising; they'd much rather be informed.

But the new wave of financial advertising seems to be a sensible compromise; it preserves the emphasis on information but injects some much needed zip. Figures 24–1 through 24–3 are some examples of quality financial advertising that meet both objectives.

Figure 24–1
Courtesy of A.G. Edwards & Sons

EXERCISE •

Financial Genius

You're the president of a new bank that's sending out invitations to prominent citizens asking them to attend your Grand Opening Celebration. What headline teaser or offer would you use on your outer envelope to entice them to open the mailing? (Giving away free money isn't allowed, just in case you were wondering.)

My Headline Teaser/Offer Is:

_____

_____

_____

_____

Helpful Hint: Think of something that was fun, enjoyable, or memorable about a party or social event you recently attended. (Hopefully, one that wasn't raided by the Vice Squad.) Now try to recreate that feeling in a headline that's equally enjoyable to read.

Figure 24–2
Courtesy of A.G. Edwards & Sons

Maybe you're not as willing to commit to a full term.

If you're always looking for the best return on your money, the last thing you

8%
Germania Bank's
Easy Access CD
$20,000 minimum deposit

may want to do is lock yourself into a CD while rates are in a state of change.
That's why a CD with no penalty for early withdrawal would make a lot of sense right now.

Leave it to Germania to create one. The Easy Access CD.

The CD that gives you the accessibility of a money market account with the high rates of a certificate of deposit. How high? As high or higher than our 30-day $100,000 CD. Guaranteed. All for as little as a $20,000 deposit.

You can make up to three withdrawals per month. And add to your account whenever you want.

Call Germania about our no penalty Easy Access CD.

After all, a long term commitment is great for someone who elects to make one.

But now you have a choice.

The Easy Access CD
Germania Bank
A Federal Savings Bank

Alton 543 E. Broadway, 465-5543/355-0700;**Alton Square** 220 E. Delmar, 465-2371; **Belleville** 6201 W. Main, 398-6850;**Cahokia** 1050 Camp Jackson Rd. 337-1555, **Dupo** 107 N. Second, 286-4582; **O'Fallon** 400 S. Lincoln Ave., 632-3615; **Springfield** 2007 S. MacArthur, 793-3550; **Normandy** 7276 Natural Bridge, 383-4311; **Downtown St. Louis** 701 Market, Suite 120, 231-0818; **Ballwin** 15061 Manchester, 227-5660; **North County** 2800 N. Highway 67, 838-3211. **FSLIC**

Minimum deposit $20,000. Individual accounts only. Rates are subject to change and are guaranteed to earn equal to or better than Germania's $100,000 CD rates through Dec., 1989.

Figure 24–3
Courtesy of TBWA Kerlick Switzer

25.

•••

Some Great Health Care Advertising

When most people think of health care advertising they tend to think of hospitals or physicians trying to attract patients. But these days health care advertising covers everything from pharmaceuticals and medical instruments to eating disorders clinics and health insurance. The good news is that highly detailed technical knowledge is seldom required to write this kind of advertising—you just have to get the right experts to give you a crash course in whatever subject you're writing about, then sift through all the facts until you have what you need.

Figures 25–1 through 25–3 are some representative examples of health care advertising from around the country.

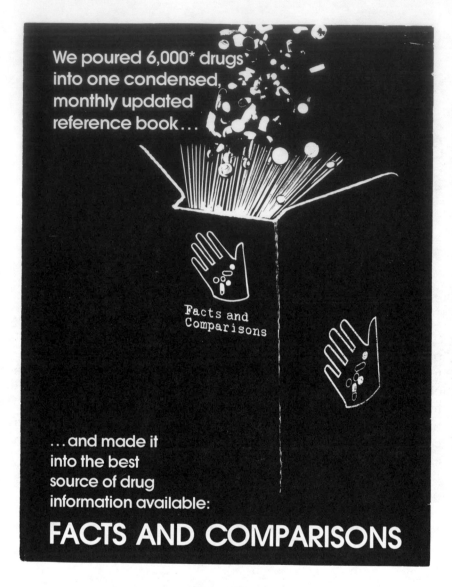

Figure 25–1
Courtesy of Ken Kroll

> # Nurses are kind and they don't laugh when you cry.
>
> ## Nursing...
> ## as explained by Jason, age 5.
>
> At CHILDREN'S HOSPITAL MEDICAL CENTER, a family-centered approach to pediatric care means our nurses participate fully in many patient experiences. They take part in the daily victories, the precious rewards. They are there to soothe a child's tears...to share a secret...to see a small face light up with laughter.
>
> But most important of all, our nurses take a fundamental role in providing state-of-the-art neonatal and pediatric care. Together with a high-caliber multidisciplinary team, they apply today's most current techniques and technologies. It is this overall dedication to excellence that has led our 341-bed facility to become one of the most renowned pediatric centers in the nation.
>
> Experience the true meaning of nursing...for further details regarding our current openings, see today's classified section. For consideration, please direct your resume in confidence to: Human Resources, Third Floor, Ambulatory Services Bldg., Elland & Bethesda Avenues, Cincinnati, OH 45229. 559-4243. An Equal Opportunity Employer M/F.
>
>
>
> Children's Hospital Medical Center

Figure 25–2
Courtesy of *Creative Newspaper* 11. Copyright 1987, The Newspaper Advertising Bureau, Inc.

Figure 25–3
Courtesy of Shoss and Associates

Q. What is BBC Health Care Facilities?

A. We are a full-service, fully staffed and equipped firm involved in planning, design and construction for the health care field. We utilize such diverse groups as designers, architects, engineers, site analysts, financial planners, construction managers, computer programmers, estimators, purchasing specialists, and more.

Q. What does "BBC" mean?

A. We are a division of Bank Building Corporation, the nation's largest designer and builder of financial facilities. It has completed more than 8,000 projects since 1913.

Q. What makes BBC Health Care Facilities different from other companies?

A. We use our own method of the design/construction management approach. Our extensive experience has shown us this is the most effective route to give you the control you need to achieve the end-product you want, and with an early-on, guaranteed maximum price.

Q. You use the "design/construction management approach"…what are the other alternatives?

A. Today's health care facilities are built under one of three widely used delivery systems. Design/construction management; architect and general contractor; or design/build. Basically they differ in the way all of the elements of the project are obtained, coordinated, supervised, compensated, and dispensed.

Q. What is your design/construction management approach?

A. This means we plan and design your facility and then manage the construction for you. Like a full-time manager, we coordinate your plans, anticipate and pre-solve problems.

and make constant adjustments and alterations to ensure a smooth work flow. We give you a total plan, total service and total overall control. We offer you many specific advantages.

Q. What are these advantages?

A. Our method provides you a number of advantages including:
1. Single source supplier
2. Early Guaranteed Maximum Price
3. Full disclosure of subcontractor bids
4. 80% savings returned on subcontractor items
5. We absorb cost overruns
6. We provide construction input during the design process
7. Three and five-year guarantees

Q. And we retain "total" overall control?

A. That's right. We work for you. And we prevent "surprises," financial or otherwise.

Q. How close is your supervision?

A. From the very start we assume the entire responsibility. Everything is held under control by a tight program of communication and information exchange between our people and yours.

When construction begins, a BBC construction superintendent lives right in your community and supervises all construction. He is your "watchdog." He carefully observes every step to make sure the work is proceeding according to plan.

Q. How much of the construction work is done by your own employees?

A. None. All work is done by subcontractors. Wherever possible, local subcontractors are used to help benefit the community.

Q. May we suggest some subcontractors to bid on our project?

A. Certainly, but we solicit bids from all interested subcontractors, not just a chosen few unless you specify differently. The subcontractors' bids are literally an "open book," and available for your personal inspection. In fact, any savings on the total of subcontractor bids below the guaranteed price are returned 80% to you at the conclusion of your project. Any cost overruns are absorbed by us entirely. As we stated, our design/construction management approach contains no secrets or unpleasant surprises.

Q. What do your services include?

A. Our services include design, engineering, construction management, and assistance in obtaining financing, regulatory approval, structuring ownership, and development services.

Q. Can you supply us a completely furnished facility?

A. Yes. If you wish, our interior designers and equipment specialists will coordinate with project architects and engineers to give you a harmonious blending of exterior and interior design and function.

Q. Do you guarantee your work?

A. Yes, and this is very important in selecting a firm to do your work. Our guarantee is unique in the industry. We're so confident of our performance and high quality, we back our projects in writing: a three-year construction warranty on minor component parts, and a five-year construction warranty on major component parts.

Q. How can I contact you?

A. Easy. Just call our Toll-Free number: **1-800-325-9573.**

Figure 25–3 (continued)

EXERCISE ••••••••••••••••••••••••••••••••

A Real Gas

Imagine that you're the advertising director of the ABC Pharmaceutical Company, and you're about to launch a new drug that will be sold exclusively to dentists. The drug offers a safer alternative to laughing gas, which many dentists use to relax their patients before dental procedures. However, laughing gas has caused side effects in certain patients with poor health, exposing the dentist to legal problems. Sketch out a rough concept for an ad that will run in the *American Dental Association Journal.*

A Description of My Visual Would Be:

_____

_____

_____

_____

My Headline Would Be:

_____

_____

_____

_____

My Optional Subhead Would Be:

_____

_____

Helpful Hint: When writing for technical or professional publications, try to put yourself in the shoes of a typical subscriber and imagine his or her problems and frustrations. As soon as you feel you have a "lock" on what those concerns are, begin writing from that perspective.

For instance, most dentists (despite all jokes to the contrary) want to control their patients' discomfort as much as possible. But many dentists stay away from laughing gas because of potential side effects and costly, time-consuming law suits. Your copy should address that concern immediately in the headline and continue to solve it in the sublead. If you were writing a complete ad, you'd continue to hammer away at how your product offers a safe alternative until the end of closing arguments and call to action.

26.

Some Great Retail Advertising

Retail advertising is a subcategory found under the broader heading of consumer advertising. Consumer advertising markets products or services, while *retail advertising promotes the particular store where you can buy or take advantage of these products or services.*

Generally, retail advertising comes in two flavors: highly refined as in the classy ad from Robinson's Department Stores in the Los Angeles area (Figure 26–1), or highly promotional as in the heavily price-oriented ad for New York Air (Figure 26–2).

The easiest way to identify most retail advertising is to look for the word "SALE" or a special offer on price or quantity. Occasionally, you'll even find a store or boutique that manages to combine the good taste of highly refined retail advertising with the good sense to push price, as shown in the ad for Shaws, a supermarket chain in Portland, Maine (Figure 26–3).

Figure 26–1
Courtesy of *Creative Newspaper* 11. Copyright 1987, The Newspaper Advertising Bureau, Inc.

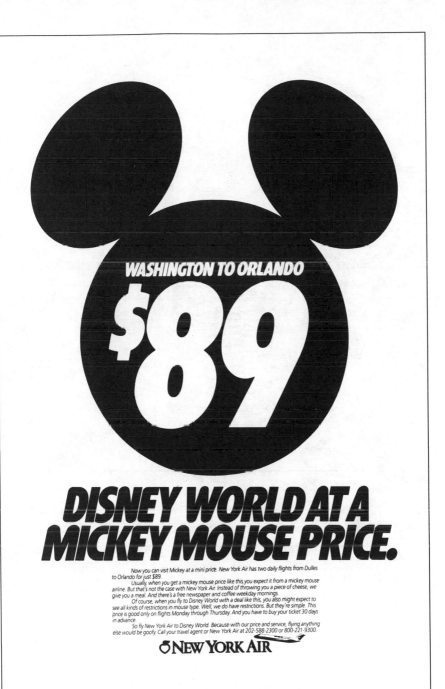

Figure 26–2

Courtesy of *Creative Newspaper* 11. Copyright 1987, The Newspaper Advertising
Bureau, Inc.

Summer tastes better when it comes from Shaw's.

Figure 26–3
Courtesy of *Creative Newspaper* 11. Copyright 1987, The Newspaper
Advertising Bureau, Inc.

EXERCISE ••••••••••••••••••••••••••••••••••

I Can Get It for You Retail

Retail Power Words

You	Announcing
Sale	Hurry
Discount	Lasts
Special	Sensational
Reduced	Fashion
Value	Glamorous
Limited time	Fantastic
Priced	Designer
Only	Marked down
Just	Extra savings
Exclusively	Best buy

Use the retail power words—or any other promotional words or phrases you think will do the job—to write a half-page newspaper ad announcing the Grand Opening of Susie's Sugar-Free Bakery. This is a special bakery that uses no sugar in any of its products. The bakery is owned by Susie, formerly a "full-figure" model who personally created all the recipes. In honor of the Grand Opening, Low Calorie Jelly Doughnuts will be on special—one dozen for $3.00.

My Headline:

_____

_____

_____

My Subhead (Optional):

_____

_____

_____

_____

My Body Copy (approximately five lines):

_____

_____

_____

_____

_____

My Closing Arguments/Call to Action (two to three lines):

_____

_____

_____

Helpful Hint: Whenever you have a relatively unique retailer like Susie's Sugar-Free Bakery, focus on the store first and the offer (the specially priced doughnuts) second. That way you'll be meeting two sales objectives at once—building awareness and selling the product. Since this is the last exercise in the book, why not let yourself get totally wild and crazy with it? Don't worry; everyone will still respect you in the morning. Maybe they'll even respect you *more.*

27.

··

Some Great
Subscription Advertising

A dvertising designed to get people to subscribe to publications is some of the best creative work you'll ever see.
That's because the advertisers usually have big budgets (enough
for one knockout glamour project) and an even bigger problem:
how to break through the competitive clutter and convince consumers their publication is more worthwhile than others.

To give you some idea of what they're up against, on any
given day, a typical consumer may be asked to subscribe to a new
children's science magazine, a travel magazine for big spenders, a
local restaurant review newsletter, a professional journal, and a
computer software club. It's no wonder that to emerge as King of
the Mailbox Jungle, a subscription (or subscription renewal) mailing will often go to great lengths to woo you—including tempting
you with high-tech premiums, gummed stickers that let you say
"Maybe" instead of "Yes," and that old favorite, a sincere promise to
"send no money now, we'll bill you later."

Figures 27–1 and 27–2 show two differing approaches to solic-
iting new subscribers for a local newspaper and a state magazine.

The Results Of Your AIDS Test Are In.

*Read the results of a special Minnesota Poll on AIDS, Sunday, February 9,
only in the Star and Tribune.*

Every Edition's An Extra.

Figure 27–1
Courtesy of *Creative Newspaper* 11. Copyright 1987, The
Newspaper Advertising Bureau, Inc.

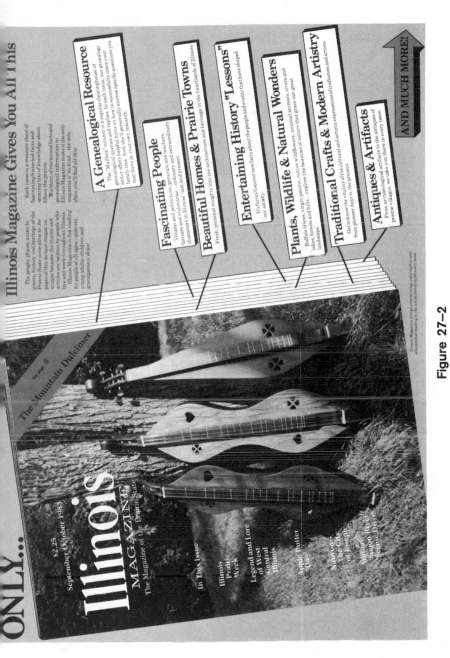

ONLY...

Illinois Magazine Gives You All This

Illinois

MAGAZINE

The Magazine of the Prairie State

$2.25
September-October 1983

In This Issue

Illinois
Prairie
Week

Legend and Lore
of West
Central
Illinois

Apple Butter
"Gang"

Naming
The Cities
of Joseph

Vandalia
Trecumseh River
Scenic Drive

The Mountain Dulcimer

The people, places, animals,
plants, history and heritage of the
Prairie State come alive in the
pages of this unique magazine. Because of this unique magazine re-
unique because the stories and
articles are written by people who
live and work throughout Illinois.
Illinois Magazine is fascinating
for people of all ages—parents,
young adults, children and
grandparents alike!

Each issue is a treasure chest of
fascinating historical facts and
amazing bits of knowledge about
life on the prairie.
The best of stories and facts and
genealogical information in
Illinois Magazine make it the only
magazine of its kind... the only
place you'll find all this:

A Genealogical Resource
The "Mailbox" column is a regular clearinghouse of
genealogical queries and replies. In each issue, our genealogy
editor offers helpful hints on how to successfully trace your
family tree. And, she'll personally answer specific questions you
may have in your own research.

Fascinating People
Villains and politicians, generals and teachers,
farmers and visionaries — ordinary and extraordinary
characters in Illinois' past and present.

Beautiful Homes & Prairie Towns
Fresh, personal insights into the architecture and heritage in the heartlands of Illinois

Entertaining History "Lessons"
It's fun to discover new facts about the people and events that have shaped
our society.

Plants, Wildlife & Natural Wonders
Buffalo traces, virgin prairie, native wildflowers, unusual animals, rivers and
lakes, forests and hills... explore the beauties of nature that grace our great
landscape.

Traditional Crafts & Modern Artistry
Get to know the vitality of the cultural and artistic expression of craftsmen and artists
from pioneer days to the present.

Antiques & Artifacts
From archaeological artifacts to the antiques of
prairie villages, we take you there in every issue.

AND MUCH MORE!

*Illinois Magazine brings patterns using, informative and
educational reading in the whole family with every issue.*

Figure 27–2

Courtesy of Shoss and Associates and Susan Christensen

167

Figure 27-2 (continued)

28.

●●●

If You Want to Write Advertising All Day . . . and Sometimes All Night: Thoughts on Becoming an Advertising Copywriter

Study the Best

The best copywriting education you can possibly get in this country is absolutely free. It's yours for the taking in the ads, brochures, and direct mail you come across every day; on the billboards you see along the highway; and on the TV spots you watch and the radio commercials you hear.

All you have to do is pay close attention to what you like— and especially to what you remember—and you'll eventually learn everything you need to know to become at least a passably good copywriter. What's Out There on Any Given Day is actually an advanced education in What Generally Works in Real-Life Advertising. And it's all just waiting for you—free. Even better, you can take the entire curriculum pass-fail without getting written permission from your instructor.

Because you'll also want to stay open to intelligent opinions (other than your own), you'll want to check out the weekly advertising "reviews" in the two advertising industry trade publications: *Advertising Age* and *Adweek.* Subscriptions to both are worth their weight in gold, even if you're counting your pennies.

However, the most important thing to do is to keep rigorously evaluating the advertising that you like . . . and that you hate. Think long and hard about why the ad, direct mail piece, or commercial works (or doesn't). And most importantly, try to imitate the examples that do succeed until you get the hang of how to do it yourself.

Write Your Best

Keep polishing your work constantly until you're satisfied you've gone as far as you can without going insane. (It's hard to write good advertising copy in the asylum—there are all those pills to swallow.)

Then put your copy aside overnight, assuming you have the luxury, and do additional fine-tuning the next morning. I've tinkered with ads years after they've been published because, when I saw them again, I cringed with embarrassment. I should have spent more time polishing them the first time around.

After you've collected a dozen or more ads, direct mail pieces, brochures, and commericals, read Maxine Paetro's excellent book on building your portfolio: *How to Put Your Book Together and Get a Job in Advertising.* It's a breezy, entertaining guide to organizing your work effectively so you can get an honest-to-goodness (or even honest-to-badness) copywriting job.

Work with the Best

Don't just take a job with anyone. Try to get into an agency (or a company) that's established a good reputation for creativity. Barring this, at least make sure they're not a bunch of hacks who crank out Zombie Zone advertising.

How can you tell if they're up to snuff—or just up to no good? When you go on a job interview ask to see *their* portfolio as well as showing them yours. Attend advertising award ceremonies around town. Network. Invite their ex-employees out to lunch. Ask them what their staff turnover rate is like and whether you can speak to someone who has recently left the company. If they turn pale and tremble, exit gracefully and don't look back.

Whatever you do, don't get caught in a situation where you're just in it for the money and all you're doing is slapping words down on a page. You'll end up hating advertising and everyone in it, including yourself, and that would be a shame since it's actually a tremendously enjoyable profession.

Get the Best Out of Life

To be a copywriter and create words and images that are zesty and alive, you have to be zesty and alive yourself. Dull people invariably end up writing dull copy.

So while you're working on honing your copywriting skills, also remember to invest in being the fullest, most interesting human being you can be. See the latest movies and plays. Travel as often as your budget allows. Subscribe to magazines that make you think—and think again. Sign up for adult education classes. Love whoever genuinely loves you. And most importantly, mingle and listen to all kinds of people, not just the attractive or impressive ones.

In short, embrace life in all its contradictions and let it embrace you back. After all, there comes a time when every copywriter—having writ—moves on. And that's when you'll probably stop and ask yourself The Meaning of It All. If you're a happy, multidimensional human being, and not just a successful copywriter, chances are you'll be able to give yourself a good answer.

Glossary of Advertising Terms

Terms Used in Print Ads, Brochures, and Direct Mail

Advertisement   A paid message in which the sponsor is identified.

Art Director   An ad agency employee responsible for designing and producing the artwork and layout for an advertisement.

Audiovisual Presentation   A presentation involving both pictures and spoken words; TV commercials, slide shows, videotapes, and films are all audiovisual presentations.

B & W   Black and white ad (as opposed to color).

Body Copy   The main portion of the reading matter.

Brand   The label by which a product is identified.

Brand Manager   A manager employed by an advertiser to take charge of the marketing and advertising of a brand.

Broadside   A one-page promotional flyer folded for mailing.

Brochure   A booklet promoting a product or service.

Bullet   A heavy dot used to separate lines or paragraphs of copy.

Business-to-Business Advertising   Advertising of products or services sold by one business to other businesses. Also called trade or industrial advertising, depending on the product or service being marketed.

Client   A company that uses the services of advertising professionals.

Collateral   Printed product information such as brochures, catalogs, and direct mail.

Consumer Advertising   Advertising of products sold to the general public.

Copy   Any word or text material for publication, broadcast, or production.

Copywriter   A person who writes advertising.

Creative Director   Ad agency employee responsible for supervising the work of copywriters, art directors, and others who produce advertising.

Direct Mail   Unsolicited advertising material delivered by mail.

Direct Response   Advertising that seeks to get orders or leads directly and immediately rather than to build an image or awareness over a period of time.

Four Color   Artwork reproduced in full color.

Freelancer   A self-employed copywriter, photographer, artist, media buyer, or other advertising professional.

Full Service Agency   An ad agency that offers its clients a full range of advertising services including creative services, media buying, planning, marketing, and research.

Image   The public's perception of a firm or a product.

Industrial Advertising   Advertising of industrial products and services.

Inquiry   A request for information made by a potential customer responding to an ad or promotion.

Inquiry Fulfillment Package   Product literature sent in response to an inquiry.

Jingle   Music and lyrics used in a commercial.

Layout   A drawing used to get a rough idea of how a finished ad, poster, or brochure will look.

Lift Letter (also called Lift Note)   A second letter included in a direct mail package, the lift letter is designed to increase response to the mailing. It is also known as a publisher's letter or pub note because it is often used in subscription solicitations.

Logo   The name and/or symbol of a company set in specially designed lettering.

Market   A portion of the population representing potential and current customers for a product or service.

Marketing   The activities companies perform to produce, distribute, promote, and sell products and services to their customers.

Marketing Communications   Communication used in marketing a product or service, including advertising, public relations, and sales promotion.

Mechanical   Type and artwork pasted up on a board for reproduction by the printer.

Media   Any method of communication that brings information, entertainment, and advertising to the public or the business community, including print, radio, and TV.

Merchandising   Activities designed to promote retail sales.

Objective   What you want to accomplish with your advertising.

Package Goods   Products wrapped or packaged by the manufacturer. Package goods are low in cost and are typically sold on store shelves.

Point of Purchase   Displays in stores designed to catch the consumers' attention.

Portfolio   A presentation folder containing samples of your work. Shown to prospective employers when you are interviewing for a job.

Premium   A gift offered to potential customers as motivation for buying a product.

Press Release (or News Release)   Written news information mailed to the media which is then disseminated to the public.

Promotion   Activities other than advertising that are used to encourage the purchase of a product or service.

Proof   A trial reproduction from a printer or photographer.

Prospect   A person with the money, authority, and desire to buy a product or service; a potential customer.

Psychographics   Statistics relating to the personalities, attitudes, and life styles of various groups of people.

Pub-set   Ads designed and typeset by the publication in which they will appear.

Public Relations   The activity of influencing the press so that they print (and broadcast) stories that promote a favorable image of a company and its products.

Reply Card   A self-addressed postcard sent with advertising material to encourage the prospect to respond.

Sales Lead   An inquiry from a qualified prospect.

Sales Promotion   A temporary marketing effort designed to generate short-term interest in the purchase of a product. Coupons, sales, discounts, premiums, sweepstakes, and contests are all examples of sales promotion.

Self-Mailer   A direct mail package that consists of a single piece. Often used as a less expensive alternative to a complete direct mail package.

Split Run Test   Two versions of an ad run in different copies of a publication (or in different sections of the same publication) to test the effectiveness of one version against the other.

Statement Stuffer   Minibrochures enclosed with invoices or other billing statements.

Strategy   How, in specific terms, you will meet the objective of your advertising.

Sweepstakes   A sales promotion in which prizes are awarded by chance and the consumer does not have to make a purchase to enter.

Tactics   Actions taken to execute your advertising strategy.

Teaser   Copy printed on the outside envelope of a direct mail package.

Trade Advertising Advertising aimed at wholesalers, distributors, sales reps, agents, and retailers rather than consumers.

Two Color An ad or sales brochure printed in two colors—usually black for definition and a second color such as blue, red, or yellow for effect.

Type Text set in lettering that can be reproduced by a printer.

Vertical Industry Publication Magazine intended for a narrow group of special interest readers. Example: *Computer Retailer Magazine.*

Abbreviations Used in TV and Radio Advertising

ANNCR—Announcer The narrator of the commercial.

CU—Close-Up An extremely tight shot in which a single object, such as a package label, dominates the screen.

LS—Long Shot A shot of a distant subject.

MS—Medium Shot A shot of the subject in the foreground, showing a substantial amount of the scenery.

SFX—Sound Effects Background sound other than human voices or musical instruments.

TS—Tight Shot A shot leaving little or no space around the subject.

VO—Voice-Over The voice of an off-camera narrator.

Storyboard Rough series of illustrations showing what a finished TV commercial will look like.

Bibliography

Bly, Bob, *Secrets of a Free-lance Writer: How to Make $85,000 a Year*. New York: Henry Holt and Company, 1988.

Bly, Bob, *Ads That Sell: How to Create Advertising That Gets Results*. Brentwood, NY: Asher Gallant Press, 1988.

Bly, Bob, *The Copywriter's Handbook, A Step-by-Step Guide to Writing Copy That Sells*. New York: Henry Holt and Company, 1985.

Foote, Cameron S., *The Fourth Medium: How to Use Promotional Literature to Increase Sales and Profits*. New York: Dow Jones Irwin, 1988.

"How to Build Sales Without a Sales Staff," *IN BUSINESS*, 1985.

Paetro, Maxine, *How to Put Your Book Together and Get a Job in Advertising*. Redding, CA: Hawthorn Books, 1980.

Wasserman, Dick, *How to Get Your First Copywriting Job in Advertising*. New York: E.P. Dutton, 1987.

White, Hooper, *How to Produce Effective TV Commercials*. Chicago: Crain Books, 1981.

Index